John William Dawson

Dawn of life

Being the history of the oldest known fossil remains and their relations to

geological time

John William Dawson

Dawn of life

Being the history of the oldest known fossil remains and their relations to geological time

ISBN/EAN: 9783337147204

Printed in Europe, USA, Canada, Australia, Japan

Cover: Foto ©Andreas Hilbeck / pixelio.de

More available books at **www.hansebooks.com**

THE DAWN OF LIFE;

BEING THE

History of the Oldest Known Fossil Remains,

AND

THEIR RELATIONS TO GEOLOGICAL TIME
AND TO THE DEVELOPMENT OF
THE ANIMAL KINGDOM.

BY

J. W. DAWSON, LL.D., F.R.S., F.G.S., Etc.,

PRINCIPAL AND VICE-CHANCELLOR OF M'GILL UNIVERSITY, MONTREAL;

AUTHOR OF

"ARCHAIA," "ACADIAN GEOLOGY," "THE STORY OF
THE EARTH AND MAN," ETC.

LONDON:

HODDER AND STOUGHTON,

27, PATERNOSTER ROW.

MDCCCLXXV

To the Memory of

SIR WILLIAM EDMOND LOGAN,

LL.D., F.R.S., F.G.S.,

THIS WORK IS DEDICATED,

Not merely as a fitting acknowledgment of his long and successful labours in the geology of those most ancient rocks, first named by him Laurentian, and which have afforded the earliest known traces of the beginning of life, but also as a tribute of sincere personal esteem and regard to the memory of one who, while he attained to the highest eminence as a student of nature, was also distinguished by his patriotism and public spirit, by the simplicity and earnestness of his character, and by the warmth of his friendships.

PREFACE.

An eminent German geologist has characterized the discovery of fossils in the Laurentian rocks of Canada as "the opening of a new era in geological science." Believing this to be no exaggeration, I have felt it to be a duty incumbent on those who have been the apostles of this new era, to make its significance as widely known as possible to all who take any interest in scientific subjects, as well as to those naturalists and geologists who may not have had their attention turned to this special topic.

The delivery of occasional lectures to popular audiences on this and kindred subjects, has convinced me that the beginning of life in the earth is a theme having attractions for all intelligent persons; while the numerous inquiries on the part of scientific students with reference to the fossils of the Eozoic age, show that the subject is yet far from being familiar to their minds. I offer no apology therefore for attempting to throw into the form of a book accessible to general readers, what is known as to the dawn of life, and cannot doubt that the present work will meet with at least as much acceptance as that in which I recently endeavoured to picture the whole series of the geological ages.

I have to acknowledge my obligations to Sir W. E. Logan for most of the Laurentian geology in the second chapter, and also for the beautiful map which he has kindly had prepared at his own expense as a contribution to the work. To Dr. Carpenter I am indebted for much information as to foraminiferal structures, and to Dr. Hunt for the chemistry of the subject. Mr. Selwyn, Director of the Geological Survey of Canada, has kindly given me access to the materials in its collections. Mr. Billings has contributed specimens and illustrations of Palæozoic Protozoa; and Mr. Weston has aided greatly by the preparation of slices for the microscope, and of photographs, as well as by assistance in collecting.

J. W. D.

McGill College, Montreal.
    April, 1875.

CONTENTS.

	PAGE
CHAPTER I. INTRODUCTORY	1
CHAPTER II. THE LAURENTIAN SYSTEM	7
NOTES:—LOGAN ON STRUCTURE OF LAURENTIAN; HUNT ON LIFE IN THE LAURENTIAN; LAURENTIAN GRAPHITE; WESTERN LAURENTIAN; METAMORPHISM. . .	24
CHAPTER III. THE HISTORY OF A DISCOVERY . . .	35
NOTES:—LOGAN ON DISCOVERY OF EOZOON, AND ON ADDITIONAL SPECIMENS	48
CHAPTER IV. WHAT IS EOZOON?	59
NOTES:—ORIGINAL DESCRIPTION; NOTE BY DR. CARPENTER; SPECIMENS FROM LONG LAKE; ADDITIONAL STRUCTURAL FACTS	76
CHAPTER V. PRESERVATION OF EOZOON . . .	93
NOTES:—HUNT ON MINERALOGY OF EOZOON; SILICIFIED FOSSILS IN SILURIAN LIMESTONES; MINERALS ASSOCIATED WITH EOZOON; GLAUCONITES. . .	115
CHAPTER VI. CONTEMPORARIES AND SUCCESSORS . .	127
NOTES:—ON STROMATOPORIDÆ; LOCALITIES OF EOZOON	165
CHAPTER VII. OPPONENTS AND OBJECTIONS . . .	169
NOTES:—OBJECTIONS AND REPLIES; HUNT ON CHEMICAL OBJECTIONS; REPLY BY DR. CARPENTER	184
CHAPTER VIII. THE DAWN-ANIMAL AS A TEACHER IN SCIENCE	207
APPENDIX . . .	235
INDEX . .	237

LIST OF ILLUSTRATIONS.

FULL PAGE ILLUSTRATIONS.

TO FACE PAGE

- I. CAPE TRINITY, FROM A PHOTOGRAPH (*Frontispiece*).
- II. MAP OF THE LAURENTIAN REGION ON THE RIVER OTTAWA   7
- III. WEATHERED SPECIMEN OF EOZOON, FROM A PHOTOGRAPH   35
- IV. RESTORATION OF EOZOON 59
- V. NATURE-PRINT OF EOZOON 93
- VI. CANALS OF EOZOON, MAGNIFIED, FROM PHOTOGRAPHS 127
- VII. NATURE-PRINT OF LARGE LAMINATED SPECIMEN . 169
- VIII. EOZOON WITH CHRYSOTILE, ETC. 207

WOODCUTS.

FIG.   PAGE

1. GENERAL SECTION 9
2. LAURENTIAN HILLS 11
3. SECTION OF LAURENTIAN 13
4. LAURENTIAN MAP 16
5. SECTION AT ST. PIERRE 22
6. SKETCH OF ROCKS AT ST. PIERRE . . . 22
7. EOZOON FROM BURGESS 36
8, 9. EOZOON FROM CALUMET . . . 39
10. CANALS OF EOZOON . . 41
11. NUMMULINE WALL 43
12. AMŒBA . 60
13. ACTINOPHRYS. 60

LIST OF ILLUSTRATIONS.

FIG.		PAGE
14.	Entosolenia	62
15.	Biloculina	62
16.	Polystomella	62
17.	Polymorphina	63
18.	Archæospherinæ	67
19.	Nummulites	73
20.	Calcarina	73
21.	Foraminiferal Rock-builders	75
21a.	Casts of Cells of Eozoon	92
22.	Modes of Mineralization	96
23.	Silurian Organic Limestone	98
24.	Wall of Eozoon penetrated with Canals	98
25.	Crinoid Infiltrated with Silicate	103
26.	Shell Infiltrated with Silicate	104
27.	Diagram of Proper Wall, etc.	106
28, 29.	Casts of Canals	107
30.	Eozoon from Tudor	111
31.	Acervuline Variety of Eozoon	135
32, 33, 34.	Archæospherinæ	137, 138
35.	Annelid Burrows	140
36.	Archæospherinæ	148
37.	Eozoon Bavaricum	149
38, 39, 40.	Archæocyathus	152, 153
41.	Archæocyathus (Structure of)	154
42.	Stromatopora	157
43.	Stromatopora (Structure of)	158
44.	Caunopora	159
45.	Cœnostroma	160
46.	Receptaculites	162
47, 48.	Receptaculites (Structure of)	163
49.	Laminæ of Eozoon	176

THE DAWN OF LIFE.

CHAPTER I.

INTRODUCTORY.

EVERY one has heard of, or ought to have heard of, *Eozoon Canadense*, the Canadian Dawn-animal, the sole fossil of the ancient Laurentian rocks of North America, the earliest known representative on our planet of those wondrous powers of animal life which culminate and unite themselves with the spirit-world in man himself. Yet few even of those to whom the name is familiar, know how much it implies, and how strange and wonderful is the story which can be evoked from this first-born of old ocean.

No one probably believes that animal life has been an eternal succession of like forms of being. We are familiar with the idea that in some way it was introduced; and most men now know, either from the testimony of Genesis or geology, or of both, that the lower forms of animal life were introduced first, and that these first living creatures had their birth in the waters, which are still the prolific mother of living things innumerable. Further, there is a general impression that it would be the most appropriate way that the great procession of animal existence should commence with the humblest types known to us, and should march on in successive bands of gradually increasing dignity and power, till man himself brings up the rear.

Do we know the first animal? Can we name it, explain its structure, and state its relations to its successors? Can we do this by inference from the succeeding types of being; and if so, do our anticipations agree with any actual reality disinterred from the earth's crust? If we could do this, either by inference or actual discovery, how strange it would be to know that we had before us even the remains of the first creature that could feel or will, and could place itself in vital relation with the great powers of inanimate nature. If we believe in a Creator, we shall feel it a solemn thing to have access to the first creature into which He breathed the breath of life. If we hold that all things have been evolved from collision of dead forces, then the first molecules of matter which took upon themselves the responsibility of living, and, aiming at the enjoyment of happiness, subjected themselves to the dread alternatives of pain and mortality, must surely evoke from us that filial reverence which we owe to the authors of our own being, if they do not involuntarily draw forth even a superstitious adoration. The veneration of the old Egyptian for his sacred animals would be a comparatively reasonable idolatry, if we could imagine any of these animals to have been the first that emerged from the domain of dead matter, and the first link in a reproductive chain of being that produced all the population of the world. Independently of any such hypotheses, all students of nature must regard with surpassing interest the first bright streaks of light that break on the long reign of primeval night and death, and presage the busy day of teeming animal existence.

No wonder then that geologists have long and earnestly groped in the rocky archives of the earth in search of some record of this patriarch of the animal kingdom. But after long and patient research, there still remained a large residuum of the oldest rocks, destitute of all traces of living beings, and designated by the hopeless name "Azoic,"—the formations destitute of remains of life, the stony records of a lifeless world. So the matter remained till the Laurentian rocks of Canada, lying at the base of these old Azoic formations, afforded forms believed to be of organic origin. The discovery was hailed with enthusiasm by those who had been prepared by previous study to receive it. It was regarded with feeble and not very intelligent faith by many more, and was met with half-concealed or open scepticism by others. It produced a copious crop of descriptive and controversial literature, but for the most part technical, and confined to scientific transactions and periodicals, read by very few except specialists. Thus, few even of geological and biological students have clear ideas of the real nature and mode of occurrence of these ancient organisms, and of their relations to better known forms of life; while the crudest and most inaccurate ideas have been current in lectures and popular books, and even in text-books, although to the minds of those really acquainted with the facts, all the disputed points have long ago been satisfactorily settled, and the true nature and affinities of Eozoon are distinctly and satisfactorily understood.

This state of things has long ceased to be desirable in the interests of science, since the settlement of the questions raised is in the highest degree important to the history of life. We cannot, it is true, affirm that Eozoon is in reality the long sought prototype of animal existence; but it is for us at present the last organic foothold, on which we can poise ourselves, that we may look back into the abyss of the infinite past, and forward to the long and varied progress of life in geological time. Its consideration, therefore, is certain, if properly entered into, to be fruitful of interesting and valuable thought, and to form the best possible introduction to the history of life in connection with geology.

It is for these reasons, and because I have been connected with this great discovery from the first, and have for the last ten years given to it an amount of labour and attention far greater than could be adequately represented by short and technical papers, that I have planned the present work. In it I propose to give a popular, yet as far as possible accurate, account of all that is known of the Dawn-animal of the Laurentian rocks of Canada. This will include, firstly: a descriptive notice of the Laurentian formation itself.

Secondly: a history of the steps which led to the discovery and proper interpretation of this ancient fossil. Thirdly: the description of Eozoon, and the explanation of the manner in which its remains have been preserved. Fourthly: inquiries as to forms of animal life, its contemporaries and immediate successors, or allied to it by zoological affinity. Fifthly: the objections which have been urged against its organic nature. And sixthly: the summing up of the lessons in science which it is fitted to teach. On these points, while I shall endeavour to state the substance of all that has been previously published, I shall bring forward many new facts illustrative of points hitherto more or less obscure, and shall endeavour so to picture these in themselves and their relations, as to give distinct and vivid impressions to the reader.

For the benefit of those who may not have access to the original memoirs, or may not have time to consult them, I shall append to the several chapters some of the technical details. These may be omitted by the general reader; but will serve to make the work more complete and useful as a book of reference.

The only preparation necessary for the unscientific reader of this work, will be some little knowledge of the division of geological time into successive ages, as represented by the diagram of formations appended to this chapter, and more full explanations may be obtained by consulting any of the numerous elementary manuals on geology, or "The Story of the Earth and Man," by the writer of the present work.

TABULAR VIEW OF THE EARTH'S GEOLOGICAL HISTORY.

Animal Kingdom.		Geological Periods.	Vegetable Kingdom.
Age of Man.	CENOZOIC, OR TERTIARY	Modern. Post-Pliocene, or Pleistocene. Pliocene. Miocene. Eocene.	Age of Angiosperms and Palms.
Age of Mammals.			
Age of Reptiles.	MESOZOIC	Cretaceous. Jurassic. Triassic.	Age of Cycads and Pines.
Age of Amphibians and Fishes.	PALÆOZOIC	Permian. Carboniferous. Erian, or Devonian. Upper Silurian. Lower Silurian, or Siluro-Cambrian. Cambrian or Primordial.	Age of Acrogens and Gymnosperms.
Age of Mollusks, Corals, and Crustaceans.			Age of Algæ.
Age of Protozoa, and dawn of Animal Life.	EOZOIC	Huronian. Upper Laurentian. Lower Laurentian.	Beginning of Age of Algæ.

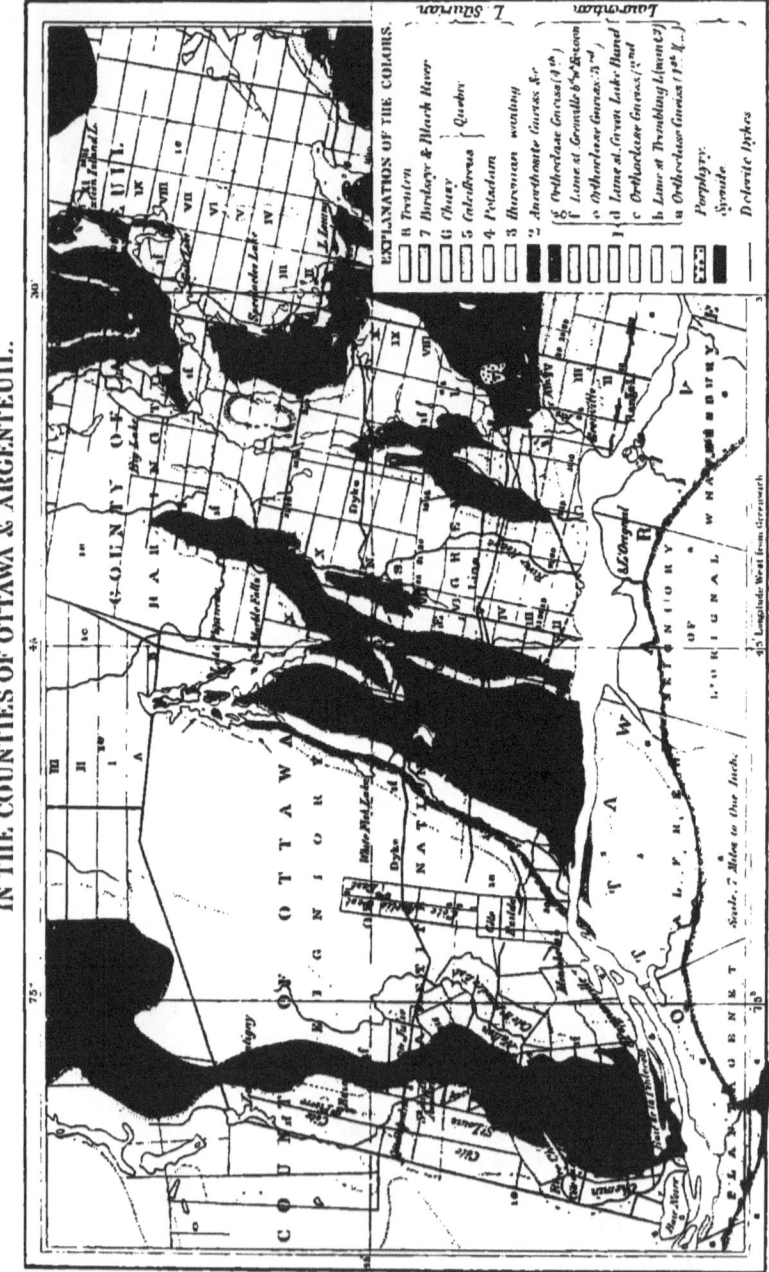

CHAPTER II.

THE LAURENTIAN ROCKS.

As we descend in depth and time into the earth's crust, after passing through nearly all the vast series of strata constituting the monuments of geological history, we at length reach the Eozoic or Laurentian rocks, deepest and oldest of all the formations known to the geologist, and more thoroughly altered or metamorphosed by heat and heated moisture than any others. These rocks, at one time known as Azoic, being supposed destitute of all remains of living things, but now more properly Eozoic, are those in which the first bright streaks of the dawn of life make their appearance.*

The name Laurentian, given originally to the Canadian development of these rocks by Sir William Logan, but now applied to them throughout the world, is derived from a range of hills lying north of the St. Lawrence valley, which the old French geographers named the Laurentides. In these hills the harder rocks of this old formation rise to considerable heights, and form the highlands separating the

* Dana has recently proposed the term "*Archæan*," on the ground that some of these rocks are as yet unfossiliferous but as the oldest known part of them contains fossils, there seems no need for this new name.

St. Lawrence valley from the great plain fronting on Hudson's Bay and the Arctic Sea. At first sight it may seem strange that rocks so ancient should anywhere appear at the surface, especially on the tops of hills; but this is a necessary result of the mode of formation of our continents. The most ancient sediments deposited in the sea were those first elevated into land, and first altered and hardened by heat. Upheaved in the folding of the earth's crust into high and rugged ridges, they have either remained uncovered with newer sediments, or have had such as were deposited on them washed away; and being of a hard and resisting nature, they have remained comparatively unworn when rocks much more modern have been swept off by denuding agencies.

But the exposure of the old Laurentian skeleton of mother earth is not confined to the Laurentide Hills, though these have given the formation its name. The same ancient rocks appear in the Adirondack mountains of New York, and in the patches which at lower levels protrude from beneath the newer formations along the American coast from Newfoundland to Maryland. The older gneisses of Norway, Sweden, and the Hebrides, of Bavaria and Bohemia, belong to the same age, and it is not unlikely that similar rocks in many other parts of the old continent will be found to be of as great antiquity. In no part of the world, however, are the Laurentian rocks more extensively distributed or better known than in North America;

and to this as the grandest and most instructive development of them, and that which first afforded organic remains, we may more especially devote our attention. Their general relations to the other formations of America may be learned from the rough generalised section (fig. 1); in which the crumpled and contorted Laurentian strata of Canada are seen to underlie unconformably the comparatively flat Silurian beds, which are themselves among the oldest monuments of the geological history of the earth.

The Laurentian rocks, associated with another series only a little younger, the Huronian, form a great belt of broken and hilly country, extending from Labrador across the north of Canada to Lake Superior, and thence bending northward to the Arctic Sea. Everywhere on the lower St. Lawrence they appear as ranges of billowy rounded ridges on the north side of the river; and as viewed from the water or the southern shore, especially when sunset deepens their tints to blue and violet, they present a grand and massive appearance, which, in the eye of the geologist,

Fig. 1. *General Section, showing the Relations of the Laurentian and Palæozoic Rocks in Canada.*
(L.) Laurentian. (1.) Cambrian, or Primordial. (2.) Lower Silurian. (3.) Upper Silurian. (4.) Devonian and Carboniferous.

who knows that they have endured the battles and the storms of time longer than any other mountains, invests them with a dignity which their mere elevation would fail to give. (Fig. 2.) In the isolated mass of the Adirondacks, south of the Canadian frontier, they rise to a still greater elevation, and form an imposing mountain group, almost equal in height to their somewhat more modern rivals, the White Mountains, which face them on the opposite side of Lake Champlain.

The grandeur of the old Laurentian ranges is, however, best displayed where they have been cut across by the great transverse gorge of the Saguenay, and where the magnificent precipices, known as Capes Trinity and Eternity, look down from their elevation of 1500 feet on a fiord, which at their base is more than 100 fathoms deep (see frontispiece). The name Eternity applied to such a mass is geologically scarcely a misnomer, for it dates back to the very dawn of geological time, and is of hoar antiquity in comparison with such upstart ranges as the Andes and the Alps.

On a nearer acquaintance, the Laurentian country appears as a broken and hilly upland and highland district, clad in its pristine state with magnificent forests, but affording few attractions to the agriculturist, except in the valleys, which follow the lines of its softer beds, while it is a favourite region for the angler, the hunter, and the lumberman. Many of the Laurentian townships of Canada

FIG. 2. *Laurentian Hills opposite Kamouraska, Lower St. Lawrence.* The islands in front are Primordial.

are, however, already extensively settled, and the traveller may pass through a succession of more or less cultivated valleys, bounded by rocks or wooded hills and crags, and diversified by running streams and romantic lakes and ponds, constituting a country always picturesque and often beautiful, and rearing a strong and hardy population. To the geologist it presents in the main immensely thick beds of gneiss, and similar metamorphic and crystalline rocks, contorted in the most remarkable manner, so that if they could be flattened out they would serve as a skin much too large for mother earth in her present state, so much has she shrunk and wrinkled since those youthful days when the Laurentian rocks were her outer covering. (Fig. 3.)

The elaborate sections of Sir William Logan show that these old rocks are divisible into two series, the Lower and Upper Laurentian; the latter being the newer of the two, and perhaps separated from the former by a long interval of time; but this Upper Laurentian being probably itself older than the Huronian series, and this again older than all the other stratified rocks. The Lower Laurentian, which attains to a thickness of more than 20,000 feet, consists of stratified granitic rocks or gneisses, of indurated sandstone or quartzite, of mica and hornblende schist, and of crystalline limestones or marbles, and iron ores, the whole interstratified with each other. The Upper Laurentian, which is 10,000 feet thick at least, consists in part of similar rocks, but associated with great beds of triclinic felspar, especially of that peculiar variety known as labradorite, or Labrador felspar, and which sometimes by its wonderful iridescent play of colours becomes a beautiful ornamental stone.

I cannot describe such rocks, but their names will tell something to those who have any knowledge of the older crystalline materials of the earth's crust. To those who have not, I would advise a visit to some cliff on the lower St. Lawrence, or the Hebridean coasts, or the shore of Norway, where the old hard crystalline and gnarled beds present their sharp edges to the ever raging sea, and show their endless alternations of various kinds and colours of strata often diversified with veins and nests of crystalline minerals. He who has seen and studied such a section of Laurentian rock cannot forget it.

All the constituents of the Laurentian series are in that state known to geologists as metamorphic. They were once sandstones, clays, and limestones, such as

FIG. 3. *Section from Petite Nation Seigniory to St. Jerome (60 miles). After Sir W. E. Logan.*

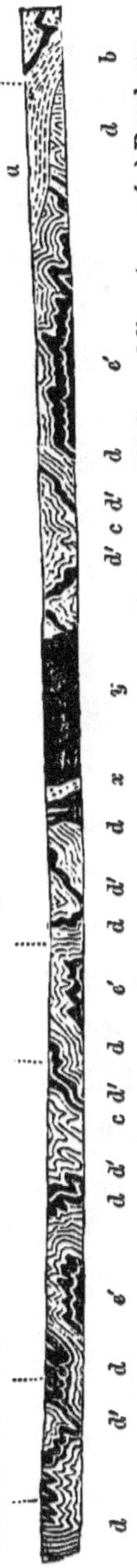

W. Petite Nation River. Eozoon. Eozoon. R. Rouge. St. Jerome. E.

(a, b.) Upper Laurentian. (c.) Fourth gneiss. (d.) Third limestone. (d'.) Third limestone. (d''.) Third gneiss. (e'.) Second limestone. (x.) Porphyry. (y.) Granite.

the sea now deposits, or such as form the common plebeian rocks of everyday plains and hills and coast sections. Being extremely old, however, they have been buried deep in the bowels of the earth under the newer deposits, and hardened by the action of pressure and of heat and heated water. Whether this heat was part of that originally belonging to the earth when a molten mass, and still existing in its interior after aqueous rocks had begun to form on its surface, or whether it is a mere mechanical effect of the intense compression which these rocks have suffered, may be a disputed question; but the observations of Sorby and of Hunt (the former in connection with the microscopic structure of rocks, and the latter in connection with the chemical conditions of change) show that no very excessive amount of heat would be required. These observations and those of Daubrée indicate that crystallization like that of the Laurentian rocks might take place at a temperature of not over $370°$ of the centigrade thermometer.

The study of those partial alterations which take place in the vicinity of volcanic and older aqueous masses of rock confirms these conclusions, so that we may be said to know the precise conditions under which sediments may be hardened into crystalline rocks, while the bedded character and the alternations of different layers in the Laurentian rocks, as well as the indications of contemporary marine life which they contain, show that they actually are such altered sediments. (See Note D.)

It is interesting to notice here that the Laurentian rocks thus interpreted show that the oldest known portions of our continents were formed in the waters. They are oceanic sediments deposited perhaps when there was no dry land or very little, and that little unknown to us except in so far as its debris may have entered into the composition of the Laurentian rocks themselves. Thus the earliest condition of the earth known to the geologist is one in which old ocean was already dominant on its surface; and any previous condition when the surface was heated, and the water constituted an abyss of vapours enveloping its surface, or any still earlier condition in which the earth was gaseous or vaporous, is a matter of mere inference, not of actual observation. The formless and void chaos is a deduction of chemical and physical principles, not a fact observed by the geologist. Still we know, from the great dykes and masses of igneous or molten rock which traverse the Laurentian beds, that even at that early period there were deep-seated fires beneath the crust; and it is quite possible that volcanic agencies then manifested themselves, not only with quite as great intensity, but also in the same manner, as at subsequent times. It is thus not unlikely that much of the land undergoing waste in the earlier Laurentian time was of the same nature with recent volcanic ejections, and that it formed groups of islands in an otherwise boundless ocean.

However this may be, the distribution and extent of these pre-Laurentian lands is, and probably ever must be, unknown to us; for it was only after the Laurentian rocks had been deposited, and after the shrinkage of the earth's crust in subsequent times had bent and contorted them, that the foundations of the continents were laid. The rude sketch map of America given in fig. 4 will show this, and will also show that the old Laurentian mountains mark out the future form of the American continent.

FIG. 4. *The Laurentian Nucleus of the American Continent.*

Rocks so highly altered as the Laurentian beds can scarcely be expected to hold well characterized fossil remains, and those geologists who entertained any hope that such remains might have been preserved, long looked in vain for their actual discovery. Still, as astronomers have suspected the existence of unknown planets from observing perturbations not accounted for, and as voyagers have suspected the approach to unknown regions by the appearance of floating wood or stray land birds, anticipations of such discoveries have been entertained and expressed from time to time. Lyell, Dana, and Sterry Hunt more especially, have committed themselves to such speculations. The reasons assigned may be stated thus:—

Assuming the Laurentian rocks to be altered sediments, they must, from their great extent, have been deposited in the ocean; and if there had been no living creatures in the waters, we have no reason to believe that they would have consisted of anything more than such sandy and muddy debris as may be washed away from wasting rocks originally of igneous origin. But the Laurentian beds contain other materials than these. No formations of any geological age include thicker or more extensive limestones. One of the beds measured by the officers of the Geological Survey, is stated to be 1500 feet in thickness, another is 1250 feet thick, and a third 750 feet; making an aggregate of 3500 feet.[*] These beds may be traced, with more or less interruption, for hundreds of miles. Whatever the origin of such limestones, it is plain that they indicate causes equal in extent, and comparable in power and duration, with those which have produced the greatest lime-

[*] Logan: *Geology of Canada*, p. 45.

stones of the later geological periods. Now, in later formations, limestone is usually an organic rock, accumulated by the slow gathering from the sea-water, or its plants, of calcareous matter, by corals, foraminifera, or shell-fish, and the deposition of their skeletons, either entire or in fragments, in the sea-bottom. The most friable chalk and the most crystalline limestones have alike been formed in this way. We know of no reason why it should be different in the Laurentian period. When, therefore, we find great and conformable beds of limestone, such as those described by Sir William Logan in the Laurentian of Canada, we naturally imagine a quiet sea-bottom, in which multitudes of animals of humble organization were accumulating limestone in their hard parts, and depositing this in gradually increasing thickness from age to age. Any attempts to account otherwise for these thick and greatly extended beds, regularly interstratified with other deposits, have so far been failures, and have arisen either from a want of comprehension of the nature and magnitude of the appearances to be explained, or from the error of mistaking the true bedded limestones for veins of calcareous spar.

The Laurentian rocks contain great quantities of carbon, in the form of graphite or plumbago. This does not occur wholly, or even principally, in veins or fissures, but in the substance of the limestone and gneiss, and in regular layers. So abundant is it, that I have estimated the amount of carbon in one division of the Lower Laurentian of the Ottawa district at an aggregate thickness of not less than twenty to thirty feet, an amount comparable with that in the true coal formation itself. Now we know of no agency existing in present or in past geological time capable of deoxidizing carbonic acid, and fixing its carbon as an ingredient in permanent rocks, except vegetable life. Unless, therefore, we suppose that there existed in the Laurentian age a vast abundance of vegetation, either in the sea or on the land, we have no means of explaining the Laurentian graphite.

The Laurentian formation contains great beds of oxide of iron, sometimes seventy feet in thickness. Here again we have an evidence of organic action; for it is the deoxidizing power of vegetable matter which has in all the later formations been the efficient cause in producing bedded deposits of iron. This is the case in modern bog and lake ores, in the clay ironstones of the coal measures, and apparently also in the great ore beds of the Silurian rocks. May not similar causes have been at work in the Laurentian period?

Any one of these reasons might, in itself, be held insufficient to prove so great and, at first sight, unlikely a conclusion as that of the existence of abundant animal and vegetable life in the Laurentian; but the concurrence of the whole in a series of deposits unquestionably marine, forms a chain of evidence so powerful that it might command belief even if no fragment of any organic and living form or structure had ever been recognised in these ancient rocks.

Such was the condition of the matter until the

existence of supposed organic remains was announced by Sir W. Logan, at the American Association for the Advancement of Science, in Springfield, in 1859; and we may now proceed to narrate the manner of this discovery, and how it has been followed up.

Before doing so, however, let us visit Eozoon in one of its haunts among the Laurentian Hills. One of the most noted repositories of its remains is the great Grenville band of limestone (see section, fig. 3, and map), the outcrop of which may be seen in our map of the country near the Ottawa, twisting itself like a great serpent in the midst of the gneissose rocks; and one of the most fruitful localities is at a place called Côte St. Pierre on this band. Landing, as I did, with Mr. Weston, of the Geological Survey, last autumn, at Papineauville, we find ourselves on the Laurentian rocks, and pass over one of the great bands of gneiss for about twelve miles, to the village of St. André Avelin. On the road we see on either hand abrupt rocky ridges, partially clad with forest, and sometimes showing on their flanks the stratification of the gneiss in very distinct parallel bands, often contorted, as if the rocks, when soft, had been wrung as a washerwoman wrings clothes. Between the hills are little irregular valleys, from which the wheat and oats have just been reaped, and the tall Indian corn and yellow pumpkins are still standing in the fields. Where not cultivated, the land is covered with a rich second growth of young maples, birches, and oaks, among which still stand the stumps and tall scathed trunks of enormous pines, which constituted the original forest. Half way we cross the Nation River, a stream nearly as large as the Tweed, flowing placidly between wooded banks, which are mirrored in its surface; but in the distance we can hear the roar of its rapids, dreaded by lumberers in their spring drivings of logs, and which we were told swallowed up five poor fellows only a few months ago. Arrived at St. André, we find a wider valley, the indication of the change to the limestone band, and along this, with the gneiss hills still in view on either hand, and often encroaching on the road, we drive for five miles more to Côte St. Pierre. At this place the lowest depression of the valley is occupied by a little pond, and, hard by, the limestone, protected by a ridge of gneiss, rises in an abrupt wooded bank by the roadside, and a little further forms a bare white promontory, projecting into the fields. Here was Mr. Lowe's original excavation, whence some of the greater blocks containing Eozoon were taken, and a larger opening made by an enterprising American on a vein of fibrous serpentine, yielding "rock cotton," for packing steam pistons and similar purposes. (Figs. 5 and 6.)

The limestone is here highly inclined and much contorted, and in all the excavations a thickness of about 100 feet of it may be exposed. It is white and crystalline, varying much however in coarseness in different bands. It is in some layers pure and white, in others it is traversed by many gray layers of gneissose and other matter, or by irregular bands and

22 THE DAWN OF LIFE.

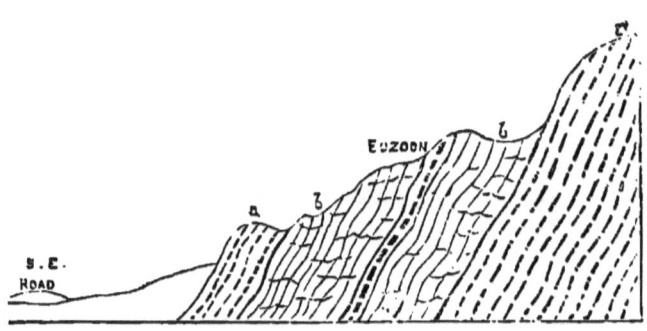

Fig. 5. *Attitude of Limestone at St. Pierre.*
(a.) Gneiss band in the Limestone. (b.) Limestone with Eozoon. (c.) Diorite and Gneiss.

Fig. 6. *Gneiss and Limestone at St. Pierre.*
(a) Limestone. (b.) Gneiss and Diorite.

nodules of pyroxene and serpentine, and it contains subordinate beds of dolomite. In one layer only, and this but a few feet thick, does the Eozoon occur in any abundance in a perfect state, though fragments and imperfectly preserved specimens abound in other parts of the bed. It is a great mistake to suppose that it constitutes whole beds of rock in an uninterrupted mass. Its true mode of occurrence is best seen on the weathered surfaces of the rock, where the serpentinous specimens project in irregular patches of various sizes, sometimes twisted by the contortion of the beds, but often too small to suffer in this way. On such surfaces the projecting patches of the fossil exhibit laminæ of serpentine so precisely like the *Stromatoporæ* of the Silurian rocks, that any collector would pounce upon them at once as fossils. In some places these small weathered specimens can be easily chipped off from the crumbling surface of the limestone; and it is perhaps to be regretted that they have not been more extensively shown to palæontologists, with the cut slices which to many of them are so problematical. One of the original specimens, brought from the Calumet, and now in the Museum of the Geological Survey of Canada, was of this kind, and much finer specimens from Côte St. Pierre are now in that collection and in my own. A very fine example is represented, on a reduced scale, in Plate III., which is taken from an original photograph.* In some of the layers are found other and more minute fossils than Eozoon,

* By Mr. Weston, of the Geological Survey of Canada.

and these, together with its fragmental remains, as ingredients in the limestone, will be discussed in the sequel. We may merely notice here that the most abundant layer of Eozoon at this place, occurs near the base of the great limestone band, and that the upper layers in so far as seen are less rich in it. Further, there is no necessary connection between Eozoon and the occurrence of serpentine, for there are many layers full of bands and lenticular masses of that mineral without any Eozoon except occasional fragments, while the fossil is sometimes partially mineralized with pyroxene, dolomite, or common limestone. The section in fig. 5 will serve to show the attitude of the limestone at this place, while the more general section, fig. 3, taken from Sir William Logan, shows its relation to the other Laurentian rocks, and the sketch in fig. 6 shows its appearance as a feature on the surface of the country.

NOTES TO CHAPTER II.

(A.) Sir William E. Logan on the Laurentian System.

[*Journal of Geological Society of London*, February, 1865.]

After stating the division of the Laurentian series into the two great groups of the Upper and Lower Laurentian, Sir William goes on to say;—

"The united thickness of these two groups in Canada cannot be less than 30,000 feet, and probably much exceeds it. The Laurentian of the west of Scotland, acording to Sir Roderick Murchison, also attains a great thickness. In that region the Upper Laurentian or Labrador series, has not yet been separately recognised; but from Mr. McCulloch's description, as well as from the specimens collected by him, and now in the Museum of the Geological Society of London, it can scarcely be doubted that the Labrador series occurs in Skye. The labradorite and hypersthene rocks from that island are identical with those of the Labrador series in Canada and New York, and unlike those of any formation at any other known horizon. This resemblance did not escape the notice of Emmons, who, in his description of the Adirondack Mountains, referred these rocks to the hypersthene rock of McCulloch, although these observers, on the opposite sides of the Atlantic, looked upon them as unstratified. In the *Canadian Naturalist* for 1862, Mr. Thomas Macfarlane, for some time resident in Norway, and now in Canada, drew attention to the striking resemblance between the Norwegian primitive gneiss formation, as described by Naumann and Keilhau, and observed by himself, and the Laurentian, including the Labrador group; and the equally remarkable similarity of the lower part of the primitive slate formation to the Huronian series, which is a third Canadian group. These primitive series attain a great thickness in the north of Europe, and constitute the main features of Scandinavian geology.

"In Bavaria and Bohemia there is an ancient gneissic series. After the labours in Scotland, by which he was the first to establish a Laurentian equivalent in the British Isles, Sir Roderick Murchison, turning his attention to this central European mass, placed it on the same horizon. These rocks, underlying Barrande's Primordial zone, with a great development of intervening clay-slate, extend southward in breadth to the banks of the Danube, with a prevailing dip towards the Silurian strata. They had previously been studied by Gümbel and Crejci, who divided them into an older reddish gneiss and a newer grey gneiss. But, on the Danube, the mass which is furthest removed from the Silurian rocks being a grey gneiss, Gümbel and Crejci account for its presence by an inverted fold in the strata; while Sir Roderick places this at the base, and regards the whole as a single series, in the normal fundamental position of the Laurentian of Scotland and of Canada.

Considering the colossal thickness given to the series (90,000 feet), it remains to be seen whether it may not include both the Lower and Upper Laurentian, and possibly, in addition, the Huronian.

"This third Canadian group (the Huronian) has been shown by my colleague, Mr. Murray, to be about 18,000 feet thick, and to consist chiefly of quartzites, slate-conglomerates, diorites, and limestones. The horizontal strata which form the base of the Lower Silurian in western Canada, rest upon the upturned edges of the Huronian series; which, in its turn, unconformably overlies the Lower Laurentian. The Huronian is believed to be more recent than the Upper Laurentian series, although the two formations have never yet been seen in contact.

"The united thickness of these three great series may possibly far surpass that of all the succeeding rocks from the base of the Palæozoic series to the present time. We are thus carried back to a period so far remote, that the appearance of the so-called Primordial fauna may by some be considered a comparatively modern event. We, however, find that, even during the Laurentian period, the same chemical and mechanical processes which have ever since been at work disintegrating and reconstructing the earth's crust were in operation as now. In the conglomerates of the Huronian series there are enclosed boulders derived from the Laurentian, which seem to show that the parent rock was altered to its present crystalline condition before the deposit of the newer formation; while interstratified with the Laurentian limestones there are beds of conglomerate, the pebbles of which are themselves rolled fragments of a still older laminated sand-rock, and the formation of these beds leads us still further into the past.

"In both the Upper and Lower Laurentian series there are several zones of limestone, each of sufficient volume to constitute an independent formation. Of these calcareous masses it has been ascertained that three, at least, belong to the Lower Laurentian. But as we do not as yet know with certainty either the base or the summit of this series, these three may be conformably followed by many more. Although the

Lower and Upper Laurentian rocks spread over more than 200,000 square miles in Canada, only about 1500 square miles have yet been fully and connectedly examined in any one district, and it is still impossible to say whether the numerous exposures of Laurentian limestone met with in other parts of the province are equivalent to any of the three zones, or whether they overlie or underlie them all."

(B.) Dr. Sterry Hunt on the Probable Existence of Life in the Laurentian Period.

Dr. Hunt's views on this subject were expressed in the *American Journal of Science,* [2], vol. xxxi., p. 395. From this article, written in 1861, after the announcement of the existence of laminated forms supposed to be organic in the Laurentian, by Sir W. E. Logan, but before their structure and affinities had been ascertained, I quote the following sentences :—

"We see in the Laurentian series beds and veins of metallic sulphurets, precisely as in more recent formations; and the extensive beds of iron ore, hundreds of feet thick, which abound in that ancient system, correspond not only to great volumes of strata deprived of that metal, but, as we may suppose, to organic matters which, but for the then great diffusion of iron-oxyd in conditions favourable for their oxidation, might have formed deposits of mineral carbon far more extensive than those beds of plumbago which we actually meet in the Laurentian strata. All these conditions lead us then to conclude the existence of an abundant vegetation during the Laurentian period.

(C.) The Graphite of the Laurentian.

The following is from a paper by the author, in the *Journal of the Geological Society,* for February, 1870:—

"The graphite of the Laurentian of Canada occurs both in beds and in veins, and in such a manner as to show that its origin and deposition are contemporaneous with those of the containing rock. Sir William Logan states* that 'the deposits of plumbago generally occur in the limestones or in their immediate vicinity, and granular varieties of the rock often contain large crystalline plates of plumbago. At other times this mineral is so finely disseminated as to give a bluish-gray colour to the limestone, and the distribution of bands thus coloured, seems to mark the stratification of the rock.' He further states:—'The plumbago is not confined to the limestones; large crystalline scales of it are occasionally disseminated in pyroxene rock or pyrallolite, and sometimes in quartzite and in feldspathic rocks, or even in magnetic oxide of iron.' In addition to these bedded forms, there are also true veins in which graphite occurs associated with calcite, quartz, orthoclase, or pyroxene, and either in disseminated scales, in detached masses, or in bands or layers 'separated from each other and from the wall rock by feldspar, pyroxene, and quartz.' Dr. Hunt also mentions the occurrence of finely granular varieties, and of that peculiarly waved and corrugated variety simulating fossil wood, though really a mere form of laminated structure, which also occurs at Warrensburgh, New York, and at the Marinski mine in Siberia. Many of the veins are not true fissures, but rather constitute a network of shrinkage cracks or segregation veins traversing in countless numbers the containing rock, and most irregular in their dimensions, so that they often resemble strings of nodular masses. It has been supposed that the graphite of the veins was originally introduced as a liquid hydrocarbon. Dr. Hunt, however, regards it as possible that it may have been in a state of aqueous solution; † but in whatever way introduced, the character of the veins indicates that in the case of the greater number of them the carbonaceous material must have been derived from the bedded rocks traversed by these veins, while there can be no doubt that the graphite found in the beds has been deposited along with the calcareous matter or muddy and sandy sediment of which these beds were originally composed.

* *Geology of Canada*, 1863.
† *Report of the Geological Survey of Canada*, 1866.

"The quantity of graphite in the Lower Laurentian series is enormous. In a recent visit to the township of Buckingham, on the Ottawa River, I examined a band of limestone believed to be a continuation of that described by Sir W. E. Logan as the Green Lake Limestone. It was estimated to amount, with some thin interstratified bands of gneiss, to a thickness of 600 feet or more, and was found to be filled with disseminated crystals of graphite and veins of the mineral to such an extent as to constitute in some places one-fourth of the whole; and making every allowance for the poorer portions, this band cannot contain in all a less vertical thickness of pure graphite than from twenty to thirty feet. In the adjoining township of Lochaber Sir W. E. Logan notices a band from twenty-five to thirty feet thick, reticulated with graphite veins to such an extent as to be mined with profit for the mineral. At another place in the same district a bed of graphite from ten to twelve feet thick, and yielding twenty per cent. of the pure material, is worked. When it is considered that graphite occurs in similar abundance at several other horizons, in beds of limestone which have been ascertained by Sir W. E. Logan to have an aggregate thickness of 3500 feet, it is scarcely an exaggeration to maintain that the quantity of carbon in the Laurentian is equal to that in similar areas of the Carboniferous system. It is also to be observed that an immense area in Canada appears to be occupied by these graphitic and Eozoon limestones, and that rich graphitic deposits exist in the continuation of this system in the State of New York, while in rocks believed to be of this age near St. John, New Brunswick, there is a very thick bed of graphitic limestone, and associated with it three regular beds of graphite, having an aggregate thickness of about five feet.*

"It may fairly be assumed that in the present world and in those geological periods with whose organic remains we are more familiar than with those of the Laurentian, there is no other source of unoxidized carbon in rocks than that furnished by organic matter, and that this has obtained its carbon in all

---

* Matthew, in *Quart. Journ. Geol. Soc.*, vol. xxi., p. 423. *Acadian Geology*, p. 662.

cases, in the first instance, from the deoxidation of carbonic acid by living plants. No other source of carbon can, I believe, be imagined in the Laurentian period. We may, however, suppose either that the graphitic matter of the Laurentian has been accumulated in beds like those of coal, or that it has consisted of diffused bituminous matter similar to that in more modern bituminous shales and bituminous and oil-bearing limestones. The beds of graphite near St. John, some of those in the gneiss at Ticonderoga in New York, and at Lochaber and Buckingham and elsewhere in Canada, are so pure and regular that one might fairly compare them with the graphitic coal of Rhode Island. These instances, however, are exceptional, and the greater part of the disseminated and vein graphite might rather be compared in its mode of occurrence to the bituminous matter in bituminous shales and limestones.

"We may compare the disseminated graphite to that which we find in those districts of Canada in which Silurian and Devonian bituminous shales and limestones have been metamorphosed and converted into graphitic rocks not dissimilar to those in the less altered portions of the Laurentian.* In like manner it seems probable that the numerous reticulating veins of graphite may have been formed by the segregation of bituminous matter into fissures and planes of least resistance, in the manner in which such veins occur in modern bituminous limestones and shales. Such bituminous veins occur in the Lower Carboniferous limestone and shale of Dorchester and Hillsborough, New Brunswick, with an arrangement very similar to that of the veins of graphite; and in the Quebec rocks of Point Levi, veins attaining to a thickness of more than a foot, are filled with a coaly matter having a transverse columnar structure, and regarded by Logan and Hunt as an altered bitumen. These palæozoic analogies would lead us to infer that the larger part of the Laurentian graphite falls under the second class of deposits above mentioned, and that, if of vegetable origin, the organic matter must have been

* Granby, Melbourne, Owl's Head, etc., *Geology of Canada*, 1863, p. 599.

thoroughly disintegrated and bituminized before it was changed into graphite. This would also give a probability that the vegetation implied was aquatic, or at least that it was accumulated under water.

"Dr. Hunt has, however, observed an indication of terrestrial vegetation, or at least of subaërial decay, in the great beds of Laurentian iron ore. These, if formed in the same manner as more modern deposits of this kind, would imply the reducing and solvent action of substances produced in the decay of plants. In this case such great ore beds as that of Hull, on the Ottawa, seventy feet thick, or that near Newborough, 200 feet thick,* must represent a corresponding quantity of vegetable matter which has totally disappeared. It may be added that similar demands on vegetable matter as a deoxidizing agent are made by the beds and veins of metallic sulphides of the Laurentian, though some of the latter are no doubt of later date than the Laurentian rocks themselves.

"It would be very desirable to confirm such conclusions as those above deduced by the evidence of actual microscopic structure. It is to be observed, however, that when, in more modern sediments, algæ have been converted into bituminous matter, we cannot ordinarily obtain any structural evidence of the origin of such bitumen, and in the graphitic slates and limestones derived from the metamorphosis of such rocks no organic structure remains. It is true that, in certain bituminous shales and limestones of the Silurian system, shreds of organic tissue can sometimes be detected, and in some cases, as in the Lower Silurian limestone of the La Cloche mountains in Canada, the pores of brachiopodous shells and the cells of corals have been penetrated by black bituminous matter, forming what may be regarded as natural injections, sometimes of much beauty. In correspondence with this, while in some Laurentian graphitic rocks, as, for instance, in the compact graphite of Clarendon, the carbon presents a curdled appearance due to segregation, and precisely similar to that of the bitumen in more modern bituminous rocks, I can detect in the graphitic limestones occasional fibrous structures which

* *Geology of Canada,* 1863.

may be remains of plants, and in some specimens vermicular lines, which I believe to be tubes of Eozoon penetrated by matter once bituminous, but now in the state of graphite.

"When palæozoic land-plants have been converted into graphite, they sometimes perfectly retain their structure. Mineral charcoal, with structure, exists in the graphitic coal of Rhode Island. The fronds of ferns, with their minutest veins perfect, are preserved in the Devonian shales of St. John, in the state of graphite; and in the same formation there are trunks of Conifers (*Dadoxylon ouangondianum*) in which the material of the cell-walls has been converted into graphite, while their cavities have been filled with calcareous spar and quartz, the finest structures being preserved quite as well as in comparatively unaltered specimens from the coal-formation.* No structures so perfect have as yet been detected in the Laurentian, though in the largest of the three graphitic beds at St. John there appear to be fibrous structures which I believe may indicate the existence of land-plants. This graphite is composed of contorted and slickensided laminæ, much like those of some bituminous shales and coarse coals; and in these there are occasional small pyritous masses which show hollow carbonaceous fibres, in some cases presenting obscure indications of lateral pores. I regard these indications, however, as uncertain; and it is not as yet fully ascertained that these beds at St. John are on the same geological horizon with the Lower Laurentian of Canada, though they certainly underlie the Primordial series of the Acadian group, and are separated from it by beds having the character of the Huronian.

"There is thus no absolute impossibility that distinct organic tissues may be found in the Laurentian graphite, if formed from land-plants, more especially if any plants existed at that time having true woody or vascular tissues; but it cannot with certainty be affirmed that such tissues have been found. It is possible, however, that in the Laurentian period the vegetation of the land may have consisted wholly

---

* *Acadian Geology*, p. 535. In calcified specimens the structures remain in the graphite after decalcification by an acid.

of cellular plants, as, for example, mosses and lichens; and if so, there would be comparatively little hope of the distinct preservation of their forms or tissues, or of our being able to distinguish the remains of land-plants from those of Algæ.

"We may sum up these facts and considerations in the following statements:—First, that somewhat obscure traces of organic structure can be detected in the Laurentian graphite; secondly, that the general arrangement and microscopic structure of the substance corresponds with that of the carbonaceous and bituminous matters in marine formations of more modern date; thirdly, that if the Laurentian graphite has been derived from vegetable matter, it has only undergone a metamorphosis similar in kind to that which organic matter in metamorphosed sediment of later age has experienced; fourthly, that the association of the graphitic matter with organic limestone, beds of iron ore, and metallic sulphides, greatly strengthens the probability of its vegetable origin; fifthly, that when we consider the immense thickness and extent of the Eozoonal and graphitic limestones and iron ore deposits of the Laurentian, if we admit the organic origin of the limestone and graphite, we must be prepared to believe that the life of that early period, though it may have existed under low forms, was most copiously developed, and that it equalled, perhaps surpassed, in its results, in the way of geological accumulation, that of any subsequent period."

(D.) WESTERN AND OTHER LAURENTIAN ROCKS, ETC.

In the map of the Laurentian nucleus of America (fig. 4,) I have not inserted the Laurentian rocks believed to exist in the Rocky Mountains and other western ranges. Their distribution is at present uncertain, as well as the date of their elevation. They may indicate an old line of Laurentian fracture or wrinkling, parallel to the west coast, and defining its direction. In the map there should be a patch of Laurentian in the north of Newfoundland, and it should be wider at the west end of lake Superior.

Full details as to the Laurentian rocks of Canada and sectional lists of their beds will be found in the *Reports of the Geological Survey*, and Dr. Hunt has discussed very fully their chemical characters and metamorphism in his *Chemical and Geological Essays*. The recent reports of Hitchcock on New Hampshire, and Hayden on the Western Territories, contain some new facts of interest. The former recognises in the White Mountain region a series of gneisses and other altered rocks of Lower Laurentian age, and, resting unconformably on these, others corresponding to the Upper Laurentian; while above the latter are other pre-silurian formations corresponding to the Huronian and probably to the Montalban series of Hunt. These facts confirm Logan's results in Canada; and Hitchcock finds many reasons to believe in the existence of life at the time of the deposition of these old rocks. Hayden's report describes granitic and gneissose rocks, probably of Laurentian age, as appearing over great areas in Colorado, Arizona, Utah, and Nevada—showing the existence of this old metamorphic floor over vast regions of Western America.

The metamorphism of these rocks does not imply any change of their constituent elements, or interference with their bedded arrangement. It consists in the alteration of the sediments by merely molecular changes re-arranging their particles so as to render them crystalline, or by chemical reactions producing new combinations of their elements. Experiment shows that the action of heat, pressure, and waters containing alkaline carbonates and silicates, would produce such changes. The amount and character of change would depend on the composition of the sediment, the heat applied, the substances in solution in the water, and the lapse of time. (See *Hunt's Essays*, p. 24.)

CHAPTER III.

THE HISTORY OF A DISCOVERY.

It is a trite remark that most discoveries are made, not by one person, but by the joint exertions of many, and that they have their preparations made often long before they actually appear. In this case the stable foundations were laid, years before the discovery of Eozoon, by the careful surveys made by Sir William Logan and his assistants, and the chemical examination of the rocks and minerals by Dr. Sterry Hunt. On the other hand, Dr. Carpenter and others in England were examining the structure of the shells of the humbler inhabitants of the modern ocean, and the manner in which the pores of their skeletons become infiltrated with mineral matter when deposited in the sea-bottom. These laborious and apparently dissimilar branches of scientific inquiry were destined to be united by a series of happy discoveries, made not fortuitously but by painstaking and intelligent observers. The discovery of the most ancient fossil was thus not the chance picking up of a rare and curious specimen. It was not likely to be found in this way; and if so found, it would have remained unnoticed and of no scientific value, but for the accumulated stores of zoological and palæontological knowledge, and the surveys previously made, whereby the age and distribution of the Laurentian rocks and the chemical conditions of their deposition and metamorphism were ascertained.

The first specimens of Eozoon ever procured, in so far as known, were collected at Burgess in Ontario by a veteran Canadian mineralogist, Dr. Wilson of Perth, and were sent to Sir William Logan as mineral specimens. Their chief interest at that time lay in the fact that certain laminæ of a dark green mineral

FIG. 7. *Eozoon mineralized by Loganite and Dolomite.*
(Collected by Dr. Wilson, of Perth.)

present in the specimens were found, on analysis by Dr. Hunt, to be composed of a new hydrous silicate, allied to serpentine, and which he named loganite: one of these specimens is represented in fig. 7. The form of this mineral was not suspected to be of organic origin. Some years after, in 1858, other specimens, differently mineralized with the minerals serpentine and pyroxone, were found by Mr. J. McMullen, an explorer in the service of the Geological Survey, in the limestone of the Grand Calumet on the River Ottawa. These seem to have at once struck Sir W. E. Logan as resembling the Silurian fossils known as *Stromatopora*, and he showed them to Mr. Billings, the palæontologist of the survey, and to the writer, with this suggestion, confirming it with the sagacious consideration that inasmuch as the Ottawa and Burgess specimens were mineralized by different substances, yet were alike in form, there was little probability that they were merely mineral or concretionary. Mr. Billings was naturally unwilling to risk his reputation in affirming the organic nature of such specimens; and my own suggestion was that they should be sliced, and examined microscopically, and that if fossils, as they presented merely concentric laminæ and no cells, they would probably prove to be protozoa rather than corals. A few slices were accordingly made, but no definite structure could be detected. Nevertheless Sir William Logan took some of the specimens to the meeting of the American Association at Springfield, in 1859, and exhibited them as possibly Laurentian fossils; but the announcement was evidently received with some incredulity. In 1862 they were exhibited by Sir William to some geological friends in London, but he remarks that "few seemed disposed to believe in their organic character, with the exception of my friend Professor Ramsay." In 1863 the General Report of the Geological Survey, summing up its work to that time, was published, under the name of the *Geology of Canada*, and in this, at page 49, will be found two figures of one of the Calumet specimens, here reproduced, and which, though unaccompanied with any specific name or technical description, were referred to as probably Laurentian fossils. (Figs. 8 and 9.)

About this time Dr. Hunt happened to mention to me, in connection with a paper on the mineralization of fossils which he was preparing, that he proposed to notice the mode of preservation of certain fossil woods and other things with which I was familiar, and that he would show me the paper in proof, in order that he might have any suggestions that occurred to me. On reading it, I observed, among other things, that he alluded to the supposed Laurentian fossils, under the impression that the organic part was represented by the serpentine or loganite, and that the calcareous matter was the filling of the chambers. I took exception to this, stating that though in the slices before examined no structure was apparent, still my impression was that the calcareous matter was the fossil, and the serpentine or loganite the filling. He said—"In that case, would it not be well to re-examine the specimens, and to try to discover which view is correct?" He mentioned at the same time that Sir William had recently shown him some new and beautiful specimens collected by Mr. Lowe, one of the explorers on the staff of the Survey, from a third locality, at Grenville, on the Ottawa. It was supposed that these might

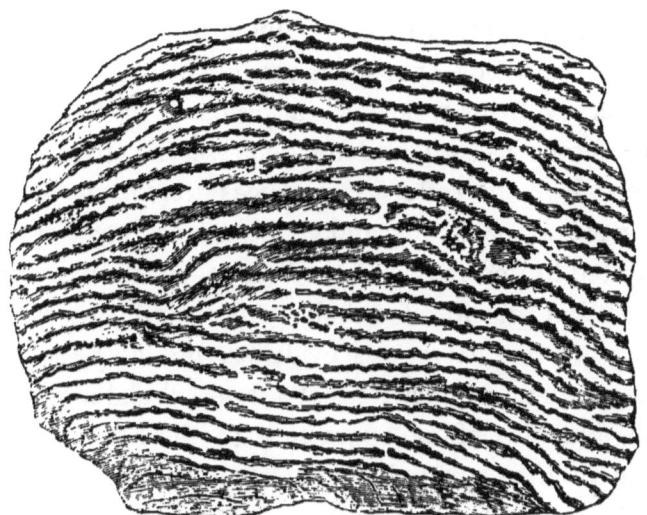

Fig. 8. *Weathered Specimen of Eozoon from the Calumet.*
(Collected by Mr. McMullen.)

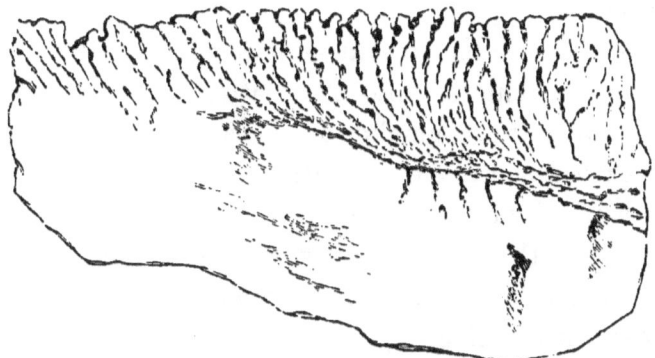

Fig. 9. *Cross Section of the Specimen represented in Fig.* 8.
The dark parts are the laminæ of calcareous matter converging to the outer surface.

throw further light on the subject; and accordingly Dr. Hunt suggested to Sir William to have additional slices of these new specimens made by Mr. Weston, of the Survey, whose skill as a preparer of these and other fossils has often done good service to science. A few days thereafter, some slices were sent to me, and were at once put under the microscope. I was delighted to find in one of the first specimens examined a beautiful group of tubuli penetrating one of the calcite layers. Here was evidence, not only that the calcite layers represented the true skeleton of the fossil, but also of its affinities with the Foraminifera, whose tubulated supplemental skeleton, as described and figured by Dr. Carpenter, and represented in specimens in my collection presented by him, was evidently of the same type with that preserved in the canals of these ancient fossils. Fig. 10 is an accurate representation of the first seen group of canals penetrated by serpentine.

On showing the structures discovered to Sir William Logan, he entered into the matter with enthusiasm, and had a great number of slices and afterwards of decalcified specimens prepared, which were placed in my hands for examination.

Feeling that the discovery was most important, but that it would be met with determined scepticism by a great many geologists, I was not content with examining the typical specimens of Eozoon, but had slices prepared of every variety of Laurentian limestone, of altered limestones from the Primordial and Silurian, and of serpentine marbles of all the varieties furnished by our collections. These were examined with ordinary and polarized light, and with every variety of illumination. Dr. Hunt, on his part, undertook the chemical investigation of the various associated minerals. An extensive series of notes and camera tracings were made of all the appearances observed;

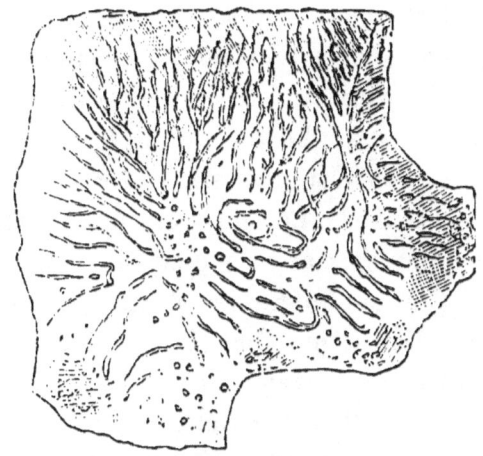

FIG. 10. *Group of Canals in the Supplemental Skeleton of Eozoon.* Taken from the specimen in which they were first recognised. Magnified.

and of some of the more important structures beautiful drawings were executed by the late Mr. H. S. Smith, the then palæontological draughtsman of the Survey. The result of the whole investigation was a firm conviction that the structure was organic and foraminiferal, and that it could be distinguished from any merely mineral or crystalline forms occurring in these or other limestones.

At this stage of the matter, and after exhibiting to Sir William all the characteristic appearances in comparison with such concretionary, dendritic, and crystalline structures as most resembled them, and also with the structure of recent and fossil Foraminifera, I suggested that the further prosecution of the matter should be handed over to Mr. Billings, as palæontologist of the Survey, and as our highest authority on the fossils of the older rocks. I was engaged in other researches, and knew that no little labour must be devoted to the work and to its publication, and that some controversy might be expected. Mr. Billings, however, with his characteristic caution and modesty, declined. His hands, he said, were full of other work, and he had not specially studied the microscopic appearances of Foraminifera or of mineral substances. It was finally arranged that I should prepare a description of the fossil, which Sir William would take to London, along with Dr. Hunt's notes, the more important specimens, and lists of the structures observed in each. Sir William was to submit the manuscript and specimens to Dr. Carpenter, or failing him to Prof. T. Rupert Jones, in the hope that these eminent authorities would confirm our conclusions, and bring forward new facts which I might have overlooked or been ignorant of. Sir William saw both gentlemen, who gave their testimony in favour of the organic and foraminiferal character of the specimens; and Dr. Carpenter in particular gave much attention to the subject, and worked out the structure of the primary cell-wall, which I had not observed previously through a curious accident as to specimens.* Mr. Lowe had been sent back to the Ottawa to explore, and just before Sir William's departure had sent in some specimens from a new locality at Petite Nation, similar in general appearance to those from Grenville, which Sir

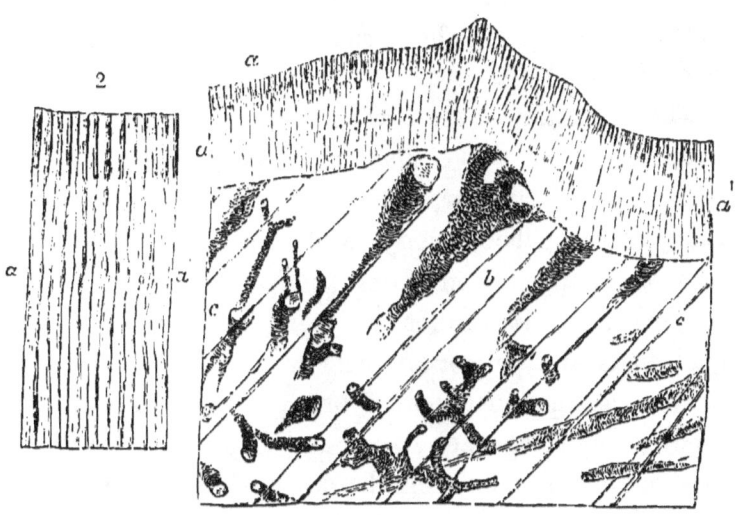

Fig. 11. *Portion of Eozoon magnified* 100 *diameters, showing the original Cell-wall with Tubulation, and the Supplemental Skeleton with Canals.* (*After Carpenter.*)

(a.) Original tubulated wall or "Nummuline layer," more magnified in fig. 2.
(b, c.) "Intermediate skeleton," with canals.

William took with him unsliced to England. These showed in a perfect manner the tubuli of the primary cell-wall, which I had in vain tried to resolve in the

* In papers by Dr. Carpenter, subsequently referred to. Prof. Jones published an able exposition of the facts in the *Popular Science Monthly.*

Grenville specimens, and which I did not see until after it had been detected by Dr. Carpenter in London. Dr. Carpenter thus contributed in a very important manner to the perfecting of the investigations begun in Canada, and on him has fallen the greater part of their illustration and defence,* in so far as Great Britain is concerned. Fig. 11, taken from one of Dr. Carpenter's papers, shows the tubulated primitive wall as described by him.

The immediate result was a composite paper in the *Proceedings of the Geological Society*, by Sir W. E. Logan, Dr. Carpenter, Dr. Hunt, and myself, in which the geology, palæontology, and mineralogy of *Eozoon Canadense* and its containing rocks were first given to the world.† It cannot be wondered at that when geologists and palæontologists were thus required to believe in the existence of organic remains in rocks regarded as altogether Azoic and hopelessly barren of fossils, and to carry back the dawn of life as far before those Primordial rocks, which were supposed to contain its first traces, as these are before the middle period of the earth's life history, some hesitation should be felt. Further, the accurate appreciation of the evidence for such a fossil as Eozoon required an amount of knowledge of minerals, of the more humble

---

* In *Quarterly Journal of Geological Society*, vol. xxii.; *Proc. Royal Society*, vol. xv.; *Intellectual Observer*, 1865. *Annals and Magazine of Natural History*, 1874; and other papers and notices.

† *Journal Geological Society*, February, 1865.

types of animals, and of the conditions of mineralization of organic remains, possessed by few even of professional geologists. Thus Eozoon has met with some negative scepticism and a little positive opposition,—though the latter has been small in amount, when we consider the novel and startling character of the facts adduced.

"The united thickness," says Sir William Logan, "of these three great series, the Lower and Upper Laurentian and Huronian, may possibly far surpass that of all succeeding rocks, from the base of the Palæozoic to the present time. We are thus carried back to a period so far remote that the appearance of the so-called Primordial fauna may be considered a comparatively modern event." So great a revolution of thought, and this based on one fossil, of a character little recognisable by geologists generally, might well tax the faith of a class of men usually regarded as somewhat faithless and sceptical. Yet this new extension of life has been generally received, and has found its way into text-books and popular treatises. Its opponents have been under the necessity of inventing the most strange and incredible pseudomorphoses of mineral substances to account for the facts; and evidently hold out rather in the spirit of adhesion to a lost cause than with any hope of ultimate success. As might have been expected, after the publication of the original paper, other facts developed themselves. Mr. Vennor found other and scarcely altered specimens in the Upper Laurentian or Huronian of Tudor.

Gümbel recognised the organism in Laurentian Rocks in Bavaria and elsewhere in Europe, and discovered a new species in the Huronian of Bavaria.* Eozoon was recognised in Laurentian limestones in Massachusetts † and New York, and there has been a rapid growth of new facts increasing our knowledge of Foraminifera of similar types in the succeeding Palæozoic rocks. Special interest attaches to the discovery by Mr. Vennor of specimens of Eozoon contained in a dark micaceous limestone at Tudor, in Ontario, and really as little metamorphosed as many Silurian fossils. Though in this state they show their minute structures less perfectly than in the serpentine specimens, the fact is most important with reference to the vindication of the animal nature of Eozoon. Another fact whose significance is not to be over-estimated, is the recognition both by Dr. Carpenter and myself of specimens in which the canals are occupied by calcite like that of the organism itself. Quite recently I have, as mentioned in the last chapter, been enabled to re-examine the locality at Petite Nation originally discovered by Mr. Lowe, and am prepared to show that all the facts with reference to the mode of occurrence of

* *Ueber das Vorkommen von Eozoon,* 1866.

† By Mr. Bicknell at Newbury, and Mr. Burbank at Chelmsford. The latter gentleman has since maintained that the limestones at the latter place are not true beds; but his own descriptions and figures, lead to the belief that this is an error of observation on his part. The Eozoon in the Chelmsford specimens and in those of Warren, New York, is in small and rare fragments in serpentinous limestone.

the forms in the beds, and their association with layers of fragmental Eozoon, are strictly in accordance with the theory that these old Laurentian limestones are truly marine deposits, holding the remains of the sea animals of their time.

Eozoon is not, however, the only witness to the great fact of Laurentian life, of which it is the most conspicuous exponent. In many of the Laurentian limestones, mixed with innumerable fragments of Eozoon, there are other fragments with traces of organic structure of a different character. There are also casts in silicious matter which seem to indicate smaller species of Foraminifera. There are besides to be summoned in evidence the enormous accumulations of carbon already referred to as existing in the Laurentian rocks, and the worm-burrows, of which very perfect traces exist in rocks probably of Upper Eozoic age.

Other discoveries also are foreshadowed here. The microscope may yet detect the true nature and affinities of some of the fragments associated with Eozoon. Less altered portions of the Laurentian rocks may be found, where even the vegetable matter may retain its organic forms, and where fossils may be recognised by their external outlines as well as by their internal structure. The Upper Laurentian and the Huronian have yet to yield up their stores of life. Thus the time may come when the rocks now called Primordial shall not be held to be so in any strict sense, and when swarming dynasties of Protozoa and other low forms of life may be known as inhabitants of oceans vastly ancient as compared with even the old Primordial seas. Who knows whether even the land of the Laurentian time may not have been clothed with plants, perhaps as much more strange and weird than those of the Devonian and Carboniferous, as those of the latter are when compared with modern forests?

NOTES TO CHAPTER III.

(A.) Sir William E. Logan on the Discovery and Characters of Eozoon.

[*Journal of Geological Society*, February, 1865.]

"In the examination of these ancient rocks, the question has often naturally occurred to me, whether during these remote periods, life had yet appeared on the earth. The apparent absence of fossils from the highly crystalline limestones did not seem to offer a proof in the negative, any more than their undiscovered presence in newer crystalline limestones where we have little doubt they have been obliterated by metamorphic action; while the carbon which, in the form of graphite, constitutes beds, or is disseminated through the calcareous or siliceous strata of the Laurentian series, seems to be an evidence of the existence of vegetation, since no one disputes the organic character of this mineral in more recent rocks. My colleague, Dr. T. Sterry Hunt, has argued for the existence of organic matters at the earth's surface during the Laurentian period from the presence of great beds of iron ore, and from the occurrence of metallic sulphurets;* and finally, the evidence was strengthened by the discovery of supposed organic forms. These were first brought to me, in October, 1858, by Mr. J. McMullen, then attached as an explorer to the

* *Quarterly Journal of the Geological Society*, xv., 493.

Geological Survey of the province, from one of the limestones of the Laurentian series occurring at the Grand Calumet, on the river Ottawa.

"Any organic remains which may have been entombed in these limestones would, if they retained their calcareous character, be almost certainly obliterated by crystallization; and it would only be by the replacement of the original carbonate of lime by a different mineral substance, or by an infiltration of such a substance into all the pores and spaces in and about the fossil, that its form would be preserved. The specimens from the Grand Calumet present parallel or apparently concentric layers resembling those of Stromatopora, except that they anastomose at various points. What were first considered the layers are composed of crystallized pyroxene, while the then supposed interstices consist of carbonate of lime. These specimens, one of which is figured in *Geology of Canada*, p. 49, called to memory others which had some years previously been obtained from Dr. James Wilson, of Perth, and were then regarded merely as minerals. They came, I believe, from masses in Burgess, but whether in place is not quite certain; and they exhibit similar forms to those of the Grand Calumet, composed of layers of a dark green magnesian silicate (loganite); while what were taken for the interstices are filled with crystalline dolomite. If the specimens from both these places were to be regarded as the result of unaided mineral arrangement, it appeared to me strange that identical forms should be derived from minerals of such different composition. I was therefore disposed to look upon them as fossils, and as such they were exhibited by me at the meeting of the American Association for the Advancement of Science, at Springfield, in August, 1859. See *Canadian Naturalist*, 1859, iv., 300. In 1862 they were shown to some of my geological friends in Great Britain; but no microscopic structure having been observed belonging to them, few seemed disposed to believe in their organic character, with the exception of my friend Professor Ramsay.

"One of the specimens had been sliced and submitted to microscopic observation, but unfortunately it was one of those composed of loganite and dolomite. In these, the minute structure is rarely seen. The true character of the specimens thus remained in suspense until last winter, when I accidentally observed indications of similar forms in blocks of Laurentian limestone which had been brought to our museum by Mr. James Lowe, one of our explorers, to be sawn up for marble. In this case the forms were composed of serpentine and calc-spar; and slices of them having been prepared for the microscope, the minute structure was observed in the first one submitted to inspection. At the request of Mr. Billings, the palæontologist of our Survey, the specimens were confided for examination and description to Dr. J. W. Dawson, of Montreal, our most practised observer with the microscope; and the conclusions at which he has arrived are appended to this communication. He finds that the serpentine, which was supposed to replace the organic form, really fills the interspaces of the calcareous fossil. This exhibits in some parts a well-preserved organic structure, which Dr. Dawson describes as that of a Foraminifer, growing in large sessile patches after the manner of Polytrema and Carpenteria, but of much larger dimensions, and presenting minute points which reveal a structure resembling that of other Foraminiferal forms, as, for example Calcarina and Nummulina.

"Dr. Dawson's description is accompanied by some remarks by Dr. Sterry Hunt on the mineralogical relations of the fossil. He observes that while the calcareous septa which form the skeleton of the Foraminifer in general remain unchanged, the sarcode has been replaced by certain silicates which have not only filled up the chambers, cells, and septal orifices, but have been injected into the minute tubuli, which are thus perfectly preserved, as may be seen by removing the calcareous matter by an acid. The replacing silicates are white pyroxene, serpentine, loganite, and pyrallolite or rensselaerite. The pyroxene and serpentine are often found in contact, filling contiguous chambers in the fossil, and were evidently formed in consecutive stages of a continuous process. In the Burgess specimens, while the sarcode is replaced by loganite, the calcareous skeleton, as has already been stated, has been replaced by dolomite, and the finer parts of the structure have been almost wholly obliterated. But in the other specimens, where the skeleton still preserves its calcareous character, the resemblance between the mode of preservation of the ancient Laurentian Foraminifera, and that of the allied forms in Tertiary and recent deposits (which, as Ehrenberg, Bailey, and Pourtales have shown, are injected with glauconite), is obvious.

"The Grenville specimens belong to the highest of the three already mentioned zones of Laurentian limestone, and it has not yet been ascertained whether the fossil extends to the two conformable lower ones, or to the calcareous zones of the overlying unconformable Upper Laurentian series. It has not yet either been determined what relation the strata from which the Burgess and Grand Calumet specimens have been obtained bear to the Grenville limestone or to one another. The zone of Grenville limestone is in some places about 1500 feet thick, and it appears to be divided for considerable distances into two or three parts by very thick bands of gneiss. One of these occupies a position towards the lower part of the limestone, and may have a volume of between 100 and 200 feet. It is at the base of the limestone that the fossil occurs. This part of the zone is largely composed of great and small irregular masses of white crystalline pyroxene, some of them twenty yards in length by four or five wide. They appear to be confusedly placed one above another, with many ragged interstices, and smoothly-worn, rounded, large and small pits and sub-cylindrical cavities, some of them pretty deep. The pyroxene, though it appears compact, presents a multitude of small spaces consisting of carbonate of lime, and many of these show minute structures similar to that of the fossil. These masses of pyroxene may characterize a thickness of about 200 feet, and the interspaces among them are filled with a mixture of serpentine and carbonate of lime. In general a sheet of pure dark green serpentine invests each mass of pyroxene; the thickness of the serpentine, varying from the sixteenth of an inch to several inches, rarely exceeding half a foot. This is followed in different spots by parallel, waving, irregularly alternating plates of carbonate of lime and serpentine, which become gradually finer as they recede from the pyroxene, and occasionally occupy a total thickness of five or six inches. These portions constitute the unbroken fossil, which may sometimes spread over an area of about a square foot, or perhaps more. Other parts, immediately on the outside of the sheet of serpentine, are occupied with about the same thickness of what appear to be the ruins of the fossil, broken up into a more or less granular mixture of calc-spar and serpentine, the former still showing minute structure; and on the outside of the whole a similar mixture appears to have been swept by currents and eddies into rudely parallel and curving layers; the mixture becoming gradually more calcareous as it recedes from the pyroxene. Sometimes beds of limestone of several feet in thickness, with the green serpentine more or less aggregated into layers, and studded with isolated lumps of pyroxene, are irregularly interstratified in the mass of rock; and less frequently there are met with lenticular patches of sandstone or granular quartzite, of a foot in thickness and several yards in diameter, holding in abundance small disseminated leaves of graphite.

"The general character of the rock connected with the fossil produces the impression that it is a great Foraminiferal reef, in which the pyroxenic masses represent a more ancient portion, which having died, and having become much broken up and worn into cavities and deep recesses, afforded a seat for a new growth of Foraminifera, represented by the calcareo-serpentinous part. This in its turn became broken up, leaving in some places uninjured portions of the general form. The main difference between this Foraminiferal reef and more recent coral-reefs seems to be that, while in the latter are usually associated many shells and other organic remains, in the more ancient one the only remains yet found are those of the animal which built the reef."

(B.) NOTE BY SIR WILLIAM E. LOGAN, ON ADDITIONAL SPECIMENS OF EOZOON.
[*Journal of Geological Society*, August, 1867.]

"Since the subject of Laurentian fossils was placed before this Society in the papers of Dr. Dawson, Dr. Carpenter, Dr.

T. Sterry Hunt, and myself, in 1865, additional specimens of Eozoon have been obtained during the explorations of the Geological Survey of Canada. These, as in the case of the specimens first discovered, have been submitted to the examination of Dr. Dawson; and it will be observed, from his remarks contained in the paper which is to follow, that one of them has afforded further, and what appears to him conclusive, evidence of their organic character. The specimens and remarks have been submitted to Dr. Carpenter, who coincides with Dr. Dawson; and the object of what I have to say in connection with these new specimens is merely to point out the localities in which they have been procured.

"The most important of these specimens was met with last summer by Mr. G. H. Vennor, one of the assistants on the Canadian Geological Survey, in the township of Tudor and county of Hastings, Ontario, about forty-five miles inland from the north shore of Lake Ontario, west of Kingston. It occurred on the surface of a layer, three inches thick, of dark grey micaceous limestone or calc-schist, near the middle of a great zone of similar rock, which is interstratified with beds of yellowish-brown sandstone, gray close grained silicious limestone, white coarsely granular limestone, and bands of dark bluish compact limestone and black pyritiferous slates, to the whole of which Mr. Vennor gives a thickness of 1000 feet. Beneath this zone are gray and pink dolomites, bluish and grayish mica slates, with conglomerates, diorites, and beds of magnetite, a red orthoclase gneiss lying at the base. The whole series, according to Mr. Vennor's section, which is appended, has a thickness of more than 12,000 feet; but the possible occurrence of more numerous folds than have hitherto been detected, may hereafter render necessary a considerable reduction.

"These measures appear to be arranged in the form of a trough, to the eastward of which, and probably beneath them, there are rocks resembling those of Grenville, from which the former differ considerably in lithological character; it is therefore supposed that the Hastings series may be somewhat higher in horizon than that of Grenville. From the village of Madoc, the zone of gray micaceous limestone, which has been particularly alluded to, runs to the eastward on one side of the trough, in a nearly vertical position into Elzivir, and on the other side to the northward, through the township of Madoc into that of Tudor, partially and unconformably overlaid in several places by horizontal beds of Lower Silurian limestone, but gradually spreading, from a diminution of the dip, from a breadth of half a mile to one of four miles. Where it thus spreads out in Tudor it becomes suddenly interrupted for a considerable part of its breadth by an isolated mass of anorthosite rock, rising about 150 feet above the general plain, and supposed to belong to the unconformable Upper Laurentian."

[Subsequent observations, however, render it probable that some of the above beds may be Huronian.]

"The Tudor limestone is comparatively unaltered: and, in the specimen obtained from it, the general form or skeleton of the fossil (consisting of white carbonate of lime) is imbedded in the limestone, without the presence of serpentine or other silicate, the colour of the skeleton contrasting strongly with that of the rock. It does not sink deep into the rock, the form having probably been loose and much abraded on what is now the under part, before being entombed. On what was the surface of the bed, the form presents a well-defined outline on one side; in this and in the arrangement of the septal layers it has a marked resemblance to the specimen first brought from the Calumet, eighty miles to the north-east, and figured in the *Geology of Canada*, p. 49; while all the forms from the Calumet, like that from Tudor, are isolated, imbedded specimens, unconnected apparently with any continuous reef, such as exists at Grenville and the Petite Nation. It will be seen, from Dr. Dawson's paper, that the minute structure is present in the Tudor specimen, though somewhat obscure; but in respect to this, strong subsidiary evidence is derived from fragments of Eozoon detected by Dr. Dawson in a specimen collected by myself from the same zone of limestone near the village of Madoc, in which the canal-system, much more distinctly displayed, is filled with carbonate of lime, as quoted from Dr. Dawson by Dr. Carpenter in the Journal of this Society for August, 1866.

"In Dr. Dawson's paper mention is made of specimens from Wentworth, and others from Long Lake. In both of these localities the rock yielding them belongs to the Grenville band, which is the uppermost of the three great bands of limestone hitherto described as interstratified in the Lower Laurentian series. That at Long Lake, situated about twenty-five miles north of Côte St. Pierre in the Petite Nation seigniory, where the best of the previous specimens were obtained, is in the direct run of the limestone there: and like it the Long Lake rock is of a serpentinous character. The locality in Wentworth occurs on Lake Louisa, about sixteen miles north of east from that of the first Grenville specimens, from which Côte St. Pierre is about the same distance north of west, the lines measuring these distances running across several important undulations in the Grenville band in both directions. The Wentworth specimens are imbedded in a portion of the Grenville band, which appears to have escaped any great alteration, and is free from serpentine, though a mixture of serpentine with white crystalline limestone occurs in the band within a mile of the spot. From this grey limestone, which has somewhat the aspect of a conglomerate, specimens have been obtained resembling some of the figures given by Gümbel in his *Illustrations* of the forms met with by him in the Laurentian rocks of Bavaria.

"In decalcifying by means of a dilute acid some of the specimens from Côte St. Pierre, placed in his hands in 1864–65, Dr. Carpenter found that the action of the acid was arrested at certain portions of the skeleton, presenting a yellowish-brown surface; and he showed me, two or three weeks ago, that in a specimen recently given him, from the same locality, considerable portions of the general form remained undissolved by such an acid. On partially reducing some of these portions to a powder, however, we immediately observed effervescence by the dilute acid; and strong acid produced it without bruising. There is little doubt that these portions of the skeleton are partially replaced by dolomite, as more recent fossils are often known to be, of which there is a noted instance in the Trenton limestone of Ottawa. But the circumstance is alluded to for the purpose of comparing these dolomitized portions of the skeleton with the specimens from Burgess, in which the replacement of the septal layers by dolomite appears to be the general condition. In such of these specimens as have been examined the minute structure seems to be wholly, or almost wholly, destroyed; but it is probable that upon a further investigation of the locality some spots will be found to yield specimens in which the calcareous skeleton still exists unreplaced by dolomite; and I may safely venture to predict that in such specimens the minute structure, in respect both to canals and tubuli, will be found as well preserved as in any of the specimens from Côte St. Pierre.

"It was the general form on weathered surfaces, and its strong resemblance to Stromatopora, which first attracted my attention to Eozoon; and the persistence of it in two distinct minerals, pyroxene and loganite, emboldened me, in 1857, to place before the Meeting of the American Association for the Advancement of Science specimens of it as probably a Laurentian fossil. After that, the form was found preserved in a third mineral, serpentine; and in one of the previous specimens it was then observed to pass continuously through two of the minerals, pyroxene and serpentine. Now we have it imbedded in limestone, just as most fossils are. In every case, with the exception of the Burgess specimens, the general form is composed of carbonate of lime; and we have good grounds for supposing it was originally so in the Burgess specimens also. If, therefore, with such evidence, and without the minute structure, I was, upon a calculation of chances, disposed, in 1857, to look upon the form as organic, much more must I so regard it when the chances have been so much augmented by the subsequent accumulation of evidence of the same kind, and the addition of the minute structure, as described by Dr. Dawson, whose observations have been confirmed and added to by the highest British authority upon the class of animals to which the form has been referred, leaving in my mind no room whatever for doubt of its organic character. Objections to it as an organism have been made by Professors King and Rowney: but these appear to me to be based upon the supposition that because some parts simulating organic structure are undoubtedly mere mineral arrangement, therefore all parts are mineral. Dr. Dawson has not proceeded upon the opposite supposition, that because some parts are, in his opinion, undoubtedly organic, therefore all parts simulating organic structure are organic; but he has carefully distinguished between the mineral and organic arrangements. I am aware, from having supplied him with a vast number of specimens prepared for the microscope by the lapidary of the Canadian Survey, from a series of rocks of Silurian and Huronian, as well as Laurentian age, and from having followed the course of his investigation as it proceeded, that nearly all the points of objection of Messrs. King and Rowney passed in review before him prior to his coming to the conclusions which he has published."

Ascending Section of the Eozoic Rocks in the County of Hastings, Ontario. By Mr. H. G. VENNOR.

	Feet.
1. Reddish and flesh-coloured granitic gneiss, the thickness of which is unknown; estimated at not less than	2,000
2. Grayish and flesh-coloured gneiss, sometimes hornblendic, passing towards the summit into a dark mica-schist, and including portions of greenish-white diorite; mean of several pretty closely agreeing measurements,	10,400
3. Crystalline limestone, sometimes magnesian, including lenticular patches of quartz, and broken and contorted layers of quartzo-felspathic rock, rarely above a few inches in thickness. This limestone, which includes in Elzivir a one-foot bed of graphite, is sometimes very thin, but in other places attains a thickness of 750 feet; estimated as averaging	400
4. Hornblendic and dioritic rocks, massive or schistose, occasionally associated near the base with dark micaceous schists, and also with chloritic and epidotic rocks, including beds of magnetite; average thickness	4,200

5. Crystalline and somewhat granular magnesian

limestone, occasionally interstratified with diorites, and near the base with silicious slates and small beds of impure steatite.. 330

This limestone, which is often silicious and ferruginous, is metalliferous, holding disseminated copper pyrites, blende, mispickel, and iron pyrites, the latter also sometimes in beds of two or three feet. Gold occurs in the limestone at the village of Madoc, associated with an argentiferous gray copper ore, and in irregular veins with bitter-spar, quartz, and a carbonaceous matter, at the Richardson mine in Madoc.

6. Gray silicious or fined-grained mica-slates, with an interstratified mass of about sixty feet of yellowish-white dolomite divided into beds by thin layers of the mica-slate, which, as well as the dolomite, often becomes conglomerate, including rounded masses of gneiss and quartzite from one to twelve inches in diameter 400

7. Bluish and grayish micaceous slate, interstratified with layers of gneiss, and occasionally holding crystals of magnetite. The whole division weathers to a rusty-brown 500

8. Gneissoid micaceous quartzites, banded gray and white, with a few instratified beds of silicious limestone, and, like the last division, weathering rusty brown 1,900

9. Gray micaceous limestone, sometimes plumbaginous, becoming on its upper portion a calc-schist, but more massive towards the base, where it is interstratified with occasional layers of diorite, and layers of a rusty-weathering gneiss like 8 1,100

This division in Tudor is traversed by numerous N.W. and S.E. veins, holding galena in a gangue of calcite and barytine. The Eozoon from Tudor here described was obtained from about the middle of this calcareous division, which appears to form the summit of the Hastings series.

Total thickness 21,130

PLATE IV.

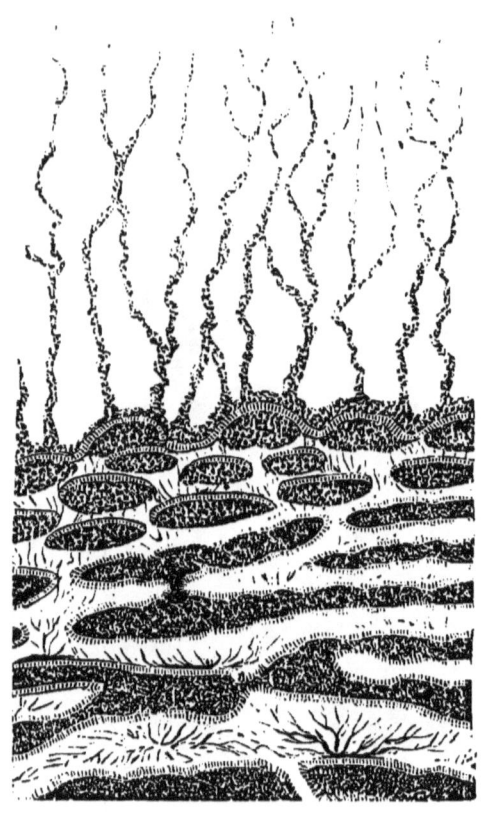

Magnified and Restored Section of a portion of Eozoon Canadense.

The portions in brown show the animal matter of the Chambers, Tubuli, Canals, and Pseudopodia; the portions uncoloured, the calcareous skeleton.

CHAPTER IV.

WHAT IS EOZOON?

THE shortest answer to this question is, that this ancient fossil is the skeleton of a creature belonging to that simple and humbly organized group of animals which are known by the name Protozoa. If we take as a familiar example of these the gelatinous and microscopic creature found in stagnant ponds, and known as the *Amœba** (fig. 12), it will form a convenient starting point. Viewed under a low power, it appears as a little patch of jelly, irregular in form, and constantly changing its aspect as it moves, by the extension of parts of its body into finger-like processes or pseudopods which serve as extempore limbs. When moving on the surface of a slip of glass under the microscope, it seems, as it were, to flow along rather than creep, and its body appears to be of a semi-fluid consistency. It may be taken as an example of the least complex forms of animal life known to us, and is often spoken of by naturalists as if it were merely a little particle of living and scarcely organized jelly or protoplasm. When minutely examined, however, it will not be found so simple as it at first sight appears. Its outer layer

* The alternating animal, alluding to its change of form.

is clear or transparent, and more dense than the inner mass, which seems granular. It has at one end a curious vesicle which can be seen gradually to expand and become filled with a clear drop of liquid, and then suddenly to contract and expel the contained fluid through a series of pores in the adjacent part of the outer wall. This is the so-called pulsating vesicle, and is an organ both of circulation and excretion. In another part of the body may be seen the nucleus,

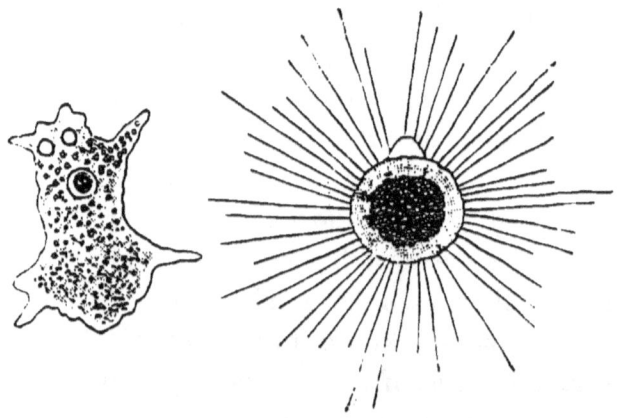

Fig. 12. *Amœba.*   Fig. 13. *Actinophrys.*
From original sketches.

which is a little cell capable, at certain times, of producing, by its division new individuals. Food when taken in through the wall of the body forms little pellets, which become surrounded by a digestive liquid exuded from the enclosing mass into rounded cavities or extemporised stomachs. Minute granules are seen to circulate in the gelatinous interior, and may be substitutes for blood-cells, and the outer layer of the body is capable of protrusion in any direction into long processes, which are very mobile, and used for locomotion and prehension. Further, this creature, though destitute of most of the parts which we are accustomed to regard as proper to animals, seems to exercise volition, and to show the same appetites and passions with animals of higher type. I have watched one of these animalcules endeavouring to swallow a one-celled plant as long as its own body; evidently hungry and eager to devour the tempting morsel, it stretched itself to its full extent, trying to envelope the object of its desire. It failed again and again; but renewed the attempt, until at length, convinced of its hopelessness, it flung itself away as if in disappointment, and made off in search of something more manageable. With the Amœba are found other types of equally simple Protozoa, but somewhat differently organized. One of these, *Actinophrys* (fig. 13), has the body globular and unchanging in form, the outer wall of greater thickness; the pulsating vesicle like a blister on the surface, and the pseudopods long and thread-like. Its habits are similar to those of the Amœba, and I introduce it to show the variations of form and structure possible even among these simple creatures.

The Amœba and Actinophrys are fresh water animals, and are destitute of any shell or covering. But in the sea there exist swarms of similar creatures, equally simple in organization, but gifted with the power of secreting around their soft bodies beautiful little shells or crusts of carbonate of lime, having one orifice, and often in

62   THE DAWN OF LIFE.

FIG. 14.   *Entosolenia.*
A one-celled Foraminifer.   Magnified as a transparent object.

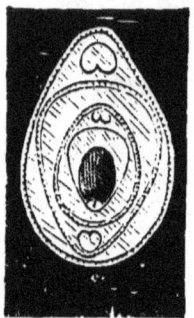

FIG. 15.   *Biloculina.*
A many-chambered Foraminifer.   Magnified as a transparent object.

FIG. 16.   *Polystomella.*
A spiral Foraminifer.   Magnified as an opaque object.

addition multitudes of microscopic pores through which the soft gelatinous matter can ooze, and form outside finger-like or thread-like extensions for collecting food. In some cases the shell consists of a single cavity only, but in most, after one cell is completed, others are added, forming a series of cells or chambers communicating with each other, and often arranged spirally or otherwise in most beautiful and symmetrical forms. Some of these creatures, usually named Foraminifera, are

Fig. 17. *Polymorphina.*

A many-chambered Foraminifer. Magnified as an opaque object. Figs. 14 to 17 are from original sketches of Post-pliocene specimens.

locomotive, others sessile and attached. Most of them are microscopic, but some grow by multiplication of chambers till they are a quarter of an inch or more in breadth. (Figs. 14 to 17.)

The original skeleton or primary cell-wall of most of these creatures is seen under the microscope to be perforated with innumerable pores, and is extremely thin. When, however, owing to the increased size of the shell, or other wants of the creature, it is necessary to give strength, this is done by adding new portions of carbonate of lime to the outside, and to these Dr. Carpenter has given the appropriate name of "supplemental skeleton;" and this, when covered by new growths, becomes what he has termed an "intermediate skeleton." The supplemental skeleton is also traversed by tubes, but these are often of larger size than the pores of the cell-wall, and of greater length, and branched in a complicated manner. (Fig. 20.) Thus there are microscopic characters by which these curious shells can be distinguished from those of other marine animals; and by applying these characters we learn that multitudes of creatures of this type have existed in former periods of the world's history, and that their shells, accumulated in the bottom of the sea, constitute large portions of many limestones. The manner in which such accumulation takes place we learn from what is now going on in the ocean, more especially from the result of the recent deep-sea dredging expeditions. The Foraminifera are vastly numerous, both near the surface and at the bottom of the sea, and multiply rapidly; and as successive generations die, their shells accumulate on the ocean bed, or are swept by currents into banks, and thus in process of time constitute thick beds of white chalky material, which may eventually be hardened into limestone. This process is now depositing a great thickness of white ooze in the bottom of the ocean; and in times past it has produced such vast thicknesses of calcareous matter as the chalk and the nummulitic limestone of Europe and the orbitoidal limestone of America. The chalk, which alone attains a maximum thickness of 1000 feet, and, according to Lyell, can be traced across Europe for 1100 geographical miles, may be said to be entirely composed of shells of Foraminifera imbedded in a paste of still more minute calcareous bodies, the Coccoliths, which are probably products of marine vegetable life, if not of some animal organism still simpler than the Foraminifera.

Lastly, we find that in the earlier geological ages there existed much larger Foraminifera than any found in our present seas; and that these, always sessile on the bottom, grew by the addition of successive chambers, in the same manner with the smaller species. To some of these we shall return in the sequel. In the meantime we shall see what claims Eozoon has to be included among them.

Let us, then, examine the structure of Eozoon, taking a typical specimen, as we find it in the limestone of Grenville or Petite Nation. In such specimens the skeleton of the animal is represented by a white crystalline marble, the cavities of the cells by green serpentine, the mode of whose introduction we shall have to consider in the sequel. The lowest layer of serpentine represents the first gelatinous coat of animal matter which grew upon the bottom, and which, if we could have seen it before any shell was formed upon its surface, must have resembled, in appearance at least, the shapeless coat of living slime found in some portions of the bed of the deep sea, which has received from

F

Huxley the name *Bathybius,* and which is believed to be a protozoon of indefinite extension, though it may possibly be merely the pulpy sarcode of sponges and similar things penetrating the ooze at their bases. On this primary layer grew a delicate calcareous shell, perforated by innumerable minute tubuli, and by some larger pores or septal orifices, while supported at intervals by perpendicular plates or pillars. Upon this again was built up, in order to strengthen it, a thickening or supplemental skeleton, more dense, and destitute of fine tubuli, but traversed by branching canals, through which the soft gelatinous matter could pass for the nourishment of the skeleton itself, and the extension of pseudopods beyond it. (Fig. 10.) So was formed the first layer of Eozoon, which seems in some cases to have spread by lateral extension over several inches of sea bottom. On this the process of growth of successive layers of animal sarcode and of calcareous skeleton was repeated again and again, till in some cases even a hundred or more layers were formed. (Photograph, Plate III., and nature print, Plate V.) As the process went on, however, the vitality of the organism became exhausted, probably by the deficient nourishment of the central and lower layers making greater and greater demands on those above, and so the succeeding layers became thinner, and less supplemental skeleton was developed. Finally, toward the top, the regular arrangement in layers was abandoned, and the cells became a mass of rounded chambers, irregularly piled up in what Dr. Carpenter has termed an "acervuline" manner, and with very thin walls unprotected by supplemental skeleton. Then the growth was arrested, and possibly these upper layers gave off reproductive germs, fitted to float or swim away and to establish new colonies. We may have such reproductive germs in certain curious globular bodies, like loose cells, found in connection with irregular Eozoon in one of the Laurentian limestones at Long Lake and elsewhere.

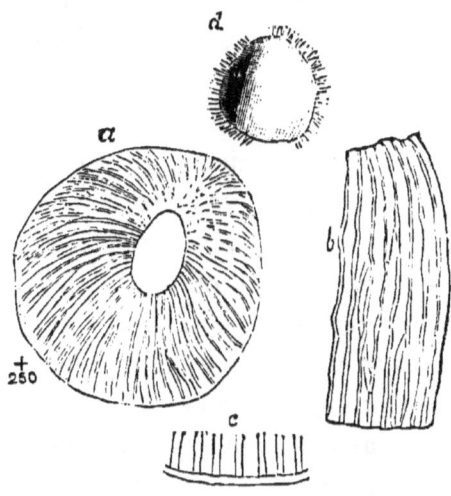

Fig. 18. *Minute Foraminiferal forms from the Laurentian of Long Lake.*

Highly magnified. (*a.*) Single cell, showing tubulated wall. (*b, c.*) Portions of same more highly magnified. (*d.*) Serpentine cast of a similar chamber, decalcified, and showing casts of tubuli.

These curious organisms I observed some years ago, but no description of them was published at the time, as I hoped to obtain better examples. I now figure some of them, and give their description in a note. (Fig. 18). I have recently obtained numerous additional examples from the beds holding Eozoon at St. Pierre, on the Ottawa. They occur at this place on the surface of layers of the limestone in vast numbers, as if they had been growing separately on the bottom, or had been drifted over it by currents. These we shall further discuss hereafter. Such was the general mode of growth of Eozoon, and we may now consider more in detail some questions as to its gigantic size, its precise mode of nutrition, the arrangement of its parts, its relations to more modern forms, and the effects of its growth in the Laurentian seas. In the meantime a study of our illustration, Plate IV., which is intended as a magnified restoration of the animal, will enable the reader distinctly to understand its structure and probable mode of growth, and to avail himself intelligently of the partial representations of its fossilised remains in the other plates and woodcuts.

With respect to its size, we shall find in a subsequent chapter that this was rivalled by some succeeding animals of the same humble type in the Silurian age; and that, as a whole, foraminiferal animals have been diminishing in size in the lapse of geological time. It is indeed a fact of so frequent occurrence that it may almost be regarded as a law of the introduction of new forms of life, that they assume in their early history gigantic dimensions, and are afterwards continued by less magnificent species. The relations of this to external conditions, in the case of higher animals, are often complex and difficult to understand; but in organisms so low as Eozoon and its allies, they lie more on the surface. Such creatures may be regarded as the simplest and most ready media for the conversion of vegetable matter into animal tissues, and their functions are almost entirely limited to those of nutrition. Hence it is likely that they will be able to appear in the most gigantic forms under such conditions as afford them the greatest amount of pabulum for the nourishment of their soft parts and for their skeletons. There is reason to believe, for example, that the occurrence, both in the chalk and the deep-sea mud, of immense quantities of the minute bodies known as Coccoliths along with Foraminifera, is not accidental. The Coccoliths appear to be grains of calcareous matter formed in minute plants adapted to a deep-sea habitat; and these, along with the vegetable and animal debris constantly being derived from the death of the living things at the surface, afford the material both of sarcode and shell. Now if the Laurentian graphite represents an exuberance of vegetable growth in those old seas proportionate to the great supplies of carbonic acid in the atmosphere and in the waters, and if the Eozoic ocean was even better supplied with carbonate of lime than those Silurian seas whose vast limestones bear testimony to their richness in such material, we can easily imagine that the conditions may have been more favourable to a creature like Eozoon than those of any other period of geological time.

Growing, as Eozoon did, on the floor of the ocean, and covering wide patches with more or less irregular masses, it must have thrown up from its whole surface its pseudopods to seize whatever floating particles of food the waters carried over it. There is also reason to believe, from the outline of certain specimens, that it often grew upward in cylindrical or club-shaped forms, and that the broader patches were penetrated by large pits or oscula, admitting the sea-water deeply into the substance of the masses. In this way its growth might be rapid and continuous; but it does not seem to have possessed the power of growing indefinitely by new and living layers covering those that had died, in the manner of some corals. Its life seems to have had a definite termination, and when that was reached an entirely new colony had to be commenced. In this it had more affinity with the Foraminifera, as we now know them, than with the corals, though practically it had the same power with the coral polyps of accumulating limestone in the sea bottom, a power indeed still possessed by its foraminiferal successors. In the case of coral limestones, we know that a large proportion of these consist not of continuous reefs but of fragments of coral mixed with other calcareous organisms, spread usually by waves and currents in continuous beds over the sea bottom. In like manner we find in the limestones containing Eozoon, layers of fragmental matter which shows in places the characteristic structures, and which evidently represents the debris swept from the Eozoic masses and reefs by the action of the waves. It is with this fragmental matter that the small rounded organisms already referred to most frequently occur; and while they may be distinct animals, they may also be the fry of Eozoon, or small portions of its acervuline upper surface floated off in a living state, and possibly capable of living independently and of founding new colonies.

It is only by a somewhat wild poetical licence that Eozoon has been represented as a "kind of enormous composite animal stretching from the shores of Labrador to Lake Superior, and thence northward and southward to an unknown distance, and forming masses 1500 feet in depth." We may discuss by-and-by the question of the composite nature of masses of Eozoon, and we see in the corals evidence of the great size to which composite animals of a higher grade can attain. In the case of Eozoon we must imagine an ocean floor more uniform and level than that now existing. On this the organism would establish itself in spots and patches. These might finally become confluent over large areas, just as massive corals do. As individual masses attained maturity and died, their pores would be filled up with limestone or silicious deposits, and thus could form a solid basis for new generations, and in this way limestone to an indefinite extent might be produced. Further, wherever such masses were high enough to be attacked by the breakers, or where portions of the sea bottom were elevated, the more fragile parts of the surface would be broken up and scattered widely in beds of fragments over the bottom of the sea, while here and there beds of mud or sand or of volcanic debris would be deposited over the living or dead organic mass, and would form the layers of gneiss and other schistose rocks interstratified with the Laurentian limestone. In this way, in short, Eozoon would perform a function combining that which corals and Foraminifera perform in the modern seas; forming both reef limestones and extensive chalky beds, and probably living both in the shallow and the deeper parts of the ocean. If in connection with this we consider the rapidity with which the soft, simple, and almost structureless sarcode of these Protozoa can be built up, and the probability that they were more abundantly supplied with food, both for nourishing their soft parts and skeletons, than any similar creatures in later times, we can readily understand the great volume and extent of the Laurentian limestones which they aided in producing. I say aided in producing, because I would not desire to commit myself to the doctrine that the Laurentian limestones are wholly of this origin. There may have been other animal limestone-builders than Eozoon, and there may have been limestones formed by plants like the modern Nullipores or by merely mineral deposition.

Its relations to modern animals of its type have been very clearly defined by Dr. Carpenter. In the structure of its proper wall and its fine parallel perforations, it resembles the *Nummulites* and their allies; and the organism may therefore be regarded as an aberrant member of the Nummuline group, which affords some of the largest and most widely distributed of the fossil Foraminifera. This resemblance may be seen in fig. 19. To the Nummulites it also conforms in its tendency to form a supplemental or intermediate skeleton with canals, though the canals themselves in their arrangement more nearly resemble Calcarina, which

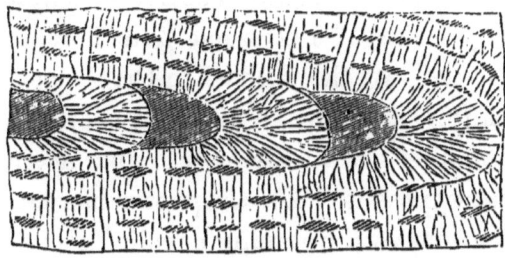

Fig. 19. *Section of a Nummulite, from Eocene Limestone of Syria.*
Showing chambers, tubuli, and canals. Compare this and fig. 20 with figs. 10 and 11.

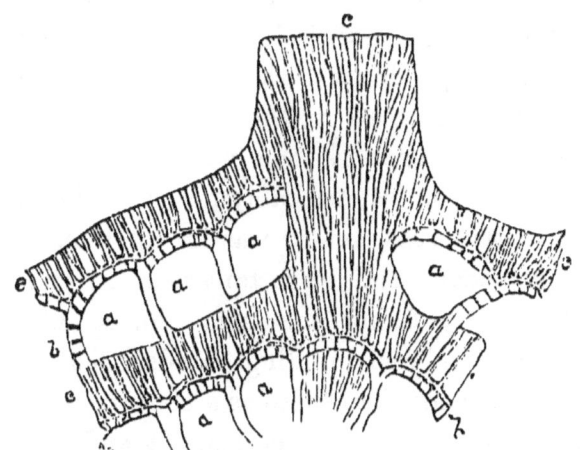

Fig. 20. *Portion of shell of Calcarina.*
Magnified, after Carpenter. (a.) Cells. (b.) Original cell-wall with tubuli. (c.) Supplementary skeleton with canals.

is represented in fig. 20. In its superposition of many layers, and in its tendency to a heaped up or acervuline irregular growth it resembles *Polytrema* and *Tinoporus*, forms of a different group in so far as shell-structure is concerned. It may thus be regarded as a composite type, combining peculiarities now observed in two groups, or it may be regarded as a representative in the Nummuline series of Polytrema and Tinoporus in the Rotaline series. At the time when Dr. Carpenter stated these affinities, it might be objected that Foraminifera of these families are in the main found in the Modern and Tertiary periods. Dr. Carpenter has since shown that the curious oval Foraminifer called *Fusulina*, found in the coal formation, is in like manner allied to both Nummulites and Rotalines; and still more recently Mr. Brady has discovered a true Nummulite in the Lower Carboniferous of Belgium. This group being now fairly brought down to the Palæozoic, we may hope finally to trace it back to the Primordial, and thus to bring it still nearer to Eozoon in time.

Though Eozoon was probably not the only animal of the Laurentian seas, yet it was in all likelihood the most conspicuous and important as a collector of calcareous matter, filling the same place afterwards occupied by the reef-building corals. Though probably less efficient than these as a constructor of solid limestones, from its less permanent and continuous growth, it formed wide floors and patches on the sea-bottom, and when these were broken up vast quantities of limestone were formed from their debris. It must also be borne in mind that Eozoon was not everywhere infiltrated with serpentine or other silicious minerals; quantities of its substance were merely filled with carbonate of lime, resembling the chamber-wall so closely that it is nearly impossible to make out the difference, and thus is likely to pass altogether unobserved by collectors, and to baffle even the microscopist. (Fig. 24.) Although therefore the layers which contain well characterized Eozoon are few and far between,

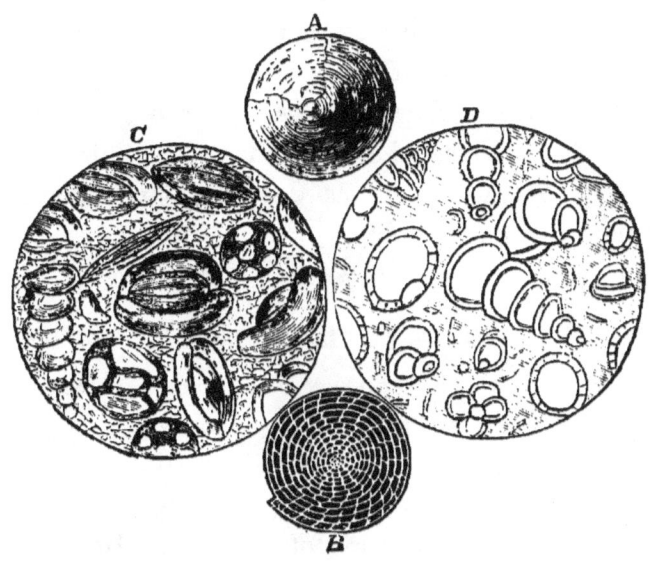

Fig. 21. *Foraminiferal Rock Builders.*

(a.) Nummulites lævigata—Eocene. (b.) The same, showing chambered interior. (c.) Milioline limestone, magnified—Eocene, Paris. (d.) Hard Chalk, section magnified—Cretaceous.

there is reason to believe that in the composition of the limestones of the Laurentian it bore no small part, and as these limestones are some of them several hundreds of feet in thickness, and extend over vast areas, Eozoon may be supposed to have been as efficient a world-builder as the Stromatoporæ of the Silurian and

Devonian, the Globigerinæ and their allies in the chalk, or the Nummulites and Miliolites in the Eocene. The two latter groups of rock-makers are represented in our cut, fig. 21; the first will engage our attention in chapter sixth. It is a remarkable illustration of the constancy of natural causes and of the persistence of animal types, that these humble Protozoans, which began to secrete calcareous matter in the Laurentian period, have been continuing their work in the ocean through all the geological ages, and are still busy in accumulating those chalky muds with which recent dredging operations in the deep sea have made us so familiar.

NOTES TO CHAPTER IV.

(A.) ORIGINAL DESCRIPTION OF EOZOON CANADENSE.

[As given by the author in the *Journal of the Geological Society*, February, 1865.]

"At the request of Sir W. E. Logan, I have submitted to microscopic examination slices of certain peculiar laminated forms, consisting of alternate layers of carbonate of lime and serpentine, and of carbonate of lime and white pyroxene, found in the Laurentian limestone of Canada, and regarded by Sir William as possibly fossils. I have also examined slices of a large number of limestones from the Laurentian series, not showing the forms of these supposed fossils.

"The specimens first mentioned are masses, often several inches in diameter, presenting to the naked eye alternate laminæ of serpentine, or of pyroxene, and carbonate of lime. Their general aspect, as remarked by Sir W. E. Logan (*Geology of Canada*, 1863, p. 49), reminds the observer of that of the Silurian corals of the genus Stromatopora, except that the laminæ diverge from and approach each other, and frequently anastomose or are connected by transverse septa.

"Under the microscope the resemblance to Stromatopora is seen to be in general form merely, and no trace appears of the radiating pillars characteristic of that genus. The laminæ of serpentine and pyroxene present no organic structure, and the latter mineral is highly crystalline. The laminæ of carbonate of lime, on the contrary, retain distinct traces of structures which cannot be of a crystalline or concretionary character. They constitute parallel or concentric partitions of variable thickness, enclosing flattened spaces or chambers, frequently crossed by transverse plates or septa, in some places so numerous as to give a vesicular appearance, in others occurring only at rare intervals. The laminæ themselves are excavated on their sides into rounded pits, and are in some places traversed by canals, or contain secondary rounded cells, apparently isolated. In addition to these general appearances, the substance of the laminæ, where most perfectly preserved, is seen to present a fine granular structure, and to be penetrated by numerous minute tubuli, which are arranged in bundles of great beauty and complexity, diverging in sheaf-like forms, and in their finer extensions anastomosing so as to form a network (figs. 10 and 28). In transverse sections, and under high powers, the tubuli are seen to be circular in outline, and sharply defined (fig. 29). In longitudinal sections, they sometimes present a beaded or jointed appearance. Even where the tubular structure is least perfectly preserved, traces of it can still be seen in most of the slices, though there are places in which the laminæ are perfectly compact, and perhaps were so originally.

"With respect to the nature and probable origin of the appearances above described, I would make the following remarks:—

"1. The serpentine and pyroxene which fill the cavities of the calcareous matter have no appearance of concretionary structure. On the contrary, their aspect is that of matter introduced by infiltration, or as sediment, and filling spaces previously existing. In other words, the calcareous matter has not been moulded on the forms of the serpentine and augite, but these have filled spaces or chambers in a hard calcareous mass. This conclusion is further confirmed by the fact, to be referred to in the sequel, that the serpentine includes multitudes of minute foreign bodies, while the calcareous matter is uniform and homogeneous. It is also to be observed that small veins of carbonate of lime occasionally traverse the specimens, and in their entire absence of structures other than crystalline, present a striking contrast to the supposed fossils.

"2. Though the calcareous laminæ have in places a crystalline cleavage, their forms and structures have no relation to this. Their cells and canals are rounded, and have smooth walls, which are occasionally lined with films apparently of carbonaceous matter. Above all, the minute tubuli are different from anything likely to occur in merely crystalline calc-spar. While in such rocks little importance might be attached to external forms simulating the appearances of corals, sponges, or other organisms, these delicate internal structures have a much higher claim to attention. Nor is there any improbability in the preservation of such minute parts in rocks so highly crystalline, since it is a circumstance of frequent occurrence in the microscopic examination of fossils that the finest structures are visible in specimens in which the general form and the arrangement of parts have been obliterated. It is also to be observed that the structure of the calcareous laminæ is the same, whether the intervening spaces are filled with serpentine or with pyroxene.

"3. The structures above described are not merely definite and uniform, but they are of a kind proper to animal organisms, and more especially to one particular type of animal life, as likely as any other to occur under such circumstances: I refer to that of the Rhizopods of the order Foraminifera. The most important point of difference is in the great size and compact habit of growth of the specimens in question; but there seems no good reason to maintain that Foraminifera must necessarily be of small size, more especially since forms of considerable magnitude referred to this type are known in the Lower Silurian. Professor Hall has described specimens of Receptaculites twelve inches in diameter; and the fossils from the Potsdam formation of Labrador, referred by Mr. Billings to the genus Archæocyathus, are examples of Protozoa with calcareous skeletons scarcely inferior in their massive style of growth to the forms now under consideration.

"These reasons are, I think, sufficient to justify me in regarding these remarkable structures as truly organic, and in searching for their nearest allies among the Foraminifera.

"Supposing then that the spaces between the calcareous laminæ, as well as the canals and tubuli traversing their substance, were once filled with the sarcode body of a Rhizopod, comparisons with modern forms at once suggest themselves.

"From the polished specimens in the Museum of the Canadian Geological Survey, it appears certain that these bodies were sessile by a broad base, and grew by the addition of successive layers of chambers separated by calcareous laminæ, but communicating with each other by canals or septal orifices sparsely and irregularly distributed. Small specimens have thus much the aspect of the modern genera Carpenteria and Polytrema. Like the first of these genera, there would also seem to have been a tendency to leave in the midst of the structure a large central canal, or deep funnel-shaped or cylindrical opening, for communication with the sea-water. Where the laminæ coalesce, and the structure becomes more vesicular, it assumes the 'acervuline' character seen in such modern forms as Nubecularia.

"Still the magnitude of these fossils is enormous when compared with the species of the genera above named; and from the specimens in the larger slabs from Grenville, in the museum of the Canadian Survey, it would seem that these organisms grew in groups, which ultimately coalesced, and formed large masses penetrated by deep irregular canals; and that they continued to grow at the surface, while the lower parts became dead and were filled up with infiltrated matter or sediment. In short, we have to imagine an organism having the habit of growth of Carpenteria, but attaining to an enormous size, and by the aggregation of individuals assuming the aspect of a coral reef.

"The complicated systems of tubuli in the Laurentian fossil indicate, however, a more complex structure than that of any of the forms mentioned above. I have carefully compared these with the similar structures in the 'supplementary skeleton' (or the shell-substance that carries the vascular system) of Calcarina and other forms, and can detect no difference except in the somewhat coarser texture of the tubuli in the Laurentian specimens. It accords well with the great dimensions of these, that they should thus thicken their walls with an extensive deposit of tubulated calcareous matter; and from the frequency of the bundles of tubuli, as well as from the thickness of the partitions, I have no doubt that all the successive walls, as they were formed, were thickened in this manner, just as in so many of the higher genera of more modern Foraminifera.

"It is proper to add that no spicules, or other structures indicating affinity to the Sponges, have been detected in any of the specimens.

"As it is convenient to have a name to designate these forms, I would propose that of Eozoon, which will be specially appropriate to what seems to be the characteristic fossil of a group of rocks which must now be named Eozoic rather than Azoic. For the species above described, the specific name of Canadense has been proposed. It may be distinguished by the following characters:—

"EOZOON CANADENSE; *gen. et spec. nov.*

"*General form.*—Massive, in large sessile patches or irregular cylinders, growing at the surface by the addition of successive laminæ.

"*Internal structure.*—Chambers large, flattened, irregular, with numerous rounded extensions, and separated by walls of variable thickness, which are penetrated by septal orifices irregularly disposed. Thicker parts of the walls with bundles of fine branching tubuli.

"These characters refer specially to the specimens from Grenville and the Calumet. There are others from Perth,

C. W., which show more regular laminæ, and in which the tubuli have not yet been observed; and a specimen from Burgess, C. W., contains some fragments of laminæ which exhibit, on one side, a series of fine parallel tubuli like those of Nummulina. These specimens may indicate distinct species; but on the other hand, their peculiarities may depend on different states of preservation.

"With respect to this last point, it may be remarked that some of the specimens from Grenville and the Calumet show the structure of the laminæ with nearly equal distinctness, whether the chambers are filled with serpentine or pyroxene, and that even the minute tubuli are penetrated and filled with these minerals. On the other hand, there are large specimens in the collection of the Canadian Survey in which the lower and still parts of the organism are imperfectly preserved in pyroxene, while the upper parts are more perfectly mineralized with serpentine."

[The following note was added in a reprint of the paper in the *Canadian Naturalist*, April, 1865.]

" Since the above was written, thick slices of Eozoon from Grenville have been prepared, and submitted to the action of hydrochloric acid until the carbonate of lime was removed. The serpentine then remains as a cast of the interior of the chambers, showing the form of their original sarcode-contents. The minute tubuli are found also to have been filled with a substance insoluble in the acid, so that casts of these also remain in great perfection, and allow their general distribution to be much better seen than in the transparent slices previously prepared. These interesting preparations establish the following additional structural points :—

" 1. That the whole mass of sarcode throughout the organism was continuous; the apparently detached secondary chambers being, as I had previously suspected, connected with the larger chambers by canals filled with sarcode.

" 2. That some of the irregular portions without lamination are not fragmentary, but due to the acervuline growth of the animal; and that this irregularity has been produced in part by the formation of projecting patches of supplementary skeleton, penetrated by beautiful systems of tubuli. These groups of tubuli are in some places very regular, and have in their axes cylinders of compact calcareous matter. Some parts of the specimens present arrangements of this kind as symmetrical as in any modern Foraminiferal shell.

"3. That all except the very thinnest portions of the walls of the chambers present traces, more or less distinct, of a tubular structure.

"4. These facts place in more strong contrast the structure of the regularly laminated species from Burgess, which do not show tubuli, and that of the Grenville specimens, less regularly laminated and tubulous throughout. I hesitated however to regard these two as distinct species, in consequence of the intermediate characters presented by specimens from the Calumet, which are regularly laminated like those of Burgess, and tubulous like those of Grenville. It is possible that in the Burgess specimens, tubuli, originally present, have been obliterated, and in organisms of this grade, more or less altered by the processes of fossilisation, large series of specimens should be compared before attempting to establish specific distinctions."

(B.) ORIGINAL DESCRIPTION OF THE SPECIMENS ADDED BY DR. CARPENTER TO THE ABOVE—IN A LETTER TO SIR W. E. LOGAN.

[*Journal of Geological Society*, February, 1865.]

"The careful examination which I have made, in accordance with the request you were good enough to convey to me from Dr. Dawson and to second on your own part, with the structure of the very extraordinary fossil which you have brought from the Laurentian rocks of Canada,* enables me most

* The specimens submitted to Dr. Carpenter were taken from a block of Eozoon rock, obtained in the Petite Nation seigniory, too late to afford Dr. Dawson an opportunity of examination. They are from the same horizon as the Grenville specimens.—W. E. L.

unhesitatingly to confirm the sagacious determination of Dr. Dawson as to its Rhizopod characters and Foraminiferal affinities, and at the same time furnishes new evidence of no small value in support of that determination. In this examination I have had the advantage of a series of sections of the fossil much superior to those submitted to Dr. Dawson; and also of a large series of decalcified specimens, of which Dr. Dawson had only the opportunity of seeing a few examples after his memoir had been written. These last are peculiarly instructive; since in consequence of the complete infiltration of the chambers and canals, originally occupied by the sarcode-body of the animal, by mineral matter insoluble in dilute nitric acid, the removal of the calcareous shell brings into view, not only the internal casts of the chambers, but also casts of the interior of the 'canal system' of the 'intermediate' or 'supplemental skeleton,' and even casts of the interior of the very fine parallel tubuli which traverse the proper walls of the chambers. And, as I have remarked elsewhere,* 'such casts place before us far more exact representations of the configuration of the animal body, and of the connections of its different parts, than we could obtain even from living specimens by dissolving away their shells with acid; its several portions being disposed to heap themselves together in a mass when they lose the support of the calcareous skeleton.'

"The additional opportunities I have thus enjoyed will be found, I believe, to account satisfactorily for the differences to be observed between Dr. Dawson's account of the Eozoon and my own. Had I been obliged to form my conclusions respecting its structure only from the specimens submitted to Dr. Dawson, I should very probably have seen no reason for any but the most complete accordance with his description: while if Dr. Dawson had enjoyed the advantage of examining the entire series of preparations which have come under my own observation, I feel confident that he would have anticipated the corrections and additions which I now offer.

"Although the general plan of growth described by Dr. Dawson, and exhibited in his photographs of vertical sections of

* *Introduction to the Study of the Foraminifera*, p. 10.

the fossil, is undoubtedly that which is typical of Eozoon, yet I find that the acervuline mode of growth, also mentioned by Dr. Dawson, very frequently takes its place in the more superficial parts, where the chambers, which are arranged in regular tiers in the laminated portions, are heaped one upon another without any regularity, as is particularly well shown in some decalcified specimens which I have myself prepared from the slices last put into my hands. I see no indication that this departure from the normal type of structure has resulted from an injury; the transition from the regular to the irregular mode of increase not being abrupt but gradual. Nor shall I be disposed to regard it as a monstrosity; since there are many other Foraminifera in which an originally definite plan of growth gives place, in a later stage, to a like acervuline piling-up of chambers.

"In regard to the form and relations of the chambers, I have little to add to Dr. Dawson's description. The evidence afforded by their internal casts concurs with that of sections, in showing that the segments of the sarcode-body, by whose aggregation each layer was constituted, were but very incompletely divided by shelly partitions; this incomplete separation (as Dr. Dawson has pointed out) having its parallel in that of the secondary chambers in Carpenteria. But I have occasionally met with instances in which the separation of the chambers has been as complete as it is in Foraminifera generally; and the communication between them is then established by several narrow passages exactly corresponding with those which I have described and figured in Cycloclypeus.*

"The mode in which each successive layer originates from the one which had preceded it, is a question to which my attention has been a good deal directed; but I do not as yet feel confident that I have been able to elucidate it completely. There is certainly no regular system of apertures for the passage of stolons giving origin to new segments, such as are found in all ordinary Polythalamous Foraminifera, whether their type of growth be rectilinear, spiral, or cyclical; and I am disposed to believe that where one layer is separated from

* Op. cit., p. 294.

another by nothing else than the proper walls of the chambers, —which, as I shall presently show, are traversed by multitudes of minute tubuli giving passage to pseudopodia,—the coalescence of these pseudopodia on the external surface would suffice to lay the foundation of a new layer of sarcodic segments. But where an intermediate or supplemental skeleton, consisting of a thick layer of solid calcareous shell, has been deposited between two successive layers, it is obvious that the animal body contained in the lower layer of chambers must be completely cut off from that which occupies the upper, unless some special provision exist for their mutual communication. Such a provision I believe to have been made by the extension of bands of sarcode, through canals left in the intermediate skeleton, from the lower to the upper tier of chambers. For in such sections as happen to have traversed thick deposits of the intermediate skeleton, there are generally found passages distinguished from those of the ordinary canal-system by their broad flat form, their great transverse diameter, and their non-ramification. One of these passages I have distinctly traced to a chamber, with the cavity of which it communicated through two or three apertures in its proper wall; and I think it likely that I should have been able to trace it at its other extremity into a chamber of the superjacent tier, had not the plane of the section passed out of its course. Riband-like casts of these passages are often to be seen in decalcified specimens, traversing the void spaces left by the removal of the thickest layers of the intermediate skeleton.

"But the organization of a new layer seems to have not unfrequently taken place in a much more considerable extension of the sarcode-body of the pre-formed layer; which either folded back its margin over the surface already consolidated, in a manner somewhat like that in which the mantle of a Cyprœa doubles back to deposit the final surface-layer of its shell, or sent upwards wall-like lamellæ, sometimes of very limited extent, but not unfrequently of considerable length, which, after traversing the substance of the shell, like trap-dykes in a bed of sandstone, spread themselves out over its surface. Such, at least, are the only interpretations I can put upon the appearances presented by decalcified specimens. For on the one hand, it is frequently to be observed that two bands of serpentine (or other infiltrated mineral), which represent two layers of the original sarcode-body of the animal, approximate to each other in some part of their course, and come into complete continuity; so that the upper layer would seem at that part to have had its origin in the lower. Again, even where these bands are most widely separated, we find that they are commonly held together by vertical lamellæ of the same material, sometimes forming mere tongues, but often running to a considerable length. That these lamellæ have not been formed by mineral infiltration into accidental fissures in the shell, but represent corresponding extensions of the sarcode-body, seems to me to be indicated not merely by the characters of their surface, but also by the fact that portions of the canal-system may be occasionally traced into connection with them.

"Although Dr. Dawson has noticed that some parts of the sections which he examined present the fine tubulation characteristic of the shells of the Nummuline Foraminifera, he does not seem to have recognised the fact, which the sections placed in my hands have enabled me most satisfactorily to determine,—that the proper walls of the chambers everywhere present the fine tubulation of the Nummuline shell; a point of the highest importance in the determination of the affinities of Eozoon. This tubulation, although not seen with the clearness with which it is to be discerned in recent examples of the Nummuline type, is here far better displayed than it is in the majority of fossil Nummulites, in which the tubuli have been filled up by the infiltration of calcareous matter, rendering the shell-substance nearly homogeneous. In Eozoön these tubuli have been filled up by the infiltration of a mineral different from that of which the shell is composed, and therefore not coalescing with it; and the tubular structure is consequently much more satisfactorily distinguishable. In decalcified specimens, the free margins of the casts of the chambers are often seen to be bordered with a delicate white glistening fringe; and when this fringe is examined with a sufficient magnifying power, it is seen to be made up of a multitude of extremely delicate aciculi, standing side by side like the fibres of asbestos. These, it is obvious, are the internal casts of the fine tubuli which perforated the proper wall of the chambers, passing directly from its inner to its outer surface; and their presence in this situation affords the most satisfactory confirmation of the evidence of that tubulation afforded by thin sections of the shell-wall.

"The successive layers, each having its own proper wall, are often superposed one upon another without the intervention of any supplemental or intermediate skeleton such as presents itself in all the more massive forms of the Nummuline series; but a deposit of this form of shell-substance, readily distinguishable by its homogeneousness from the finely tubular shell immediately investing the segments of the sarcode-body, is the source of the great thickening which the calcareous zones often present in vertical sections of Eozoon. The presence of this intermediate skeleton has been correctly indicated by Dr. Dawson; but he does not seem to have clearly differentiated it from the proper wall of the chambers. All the tubuli which he has described belong to that canal system which, as I have shown,* is limited in its distribution to the intermediate skeleton, and is expressly designed to supply a channel for its nutrition and augmentation. Of this canal system, which presents most remarkable varieties in dimensions and distribution, we learn more from the casts presented by decalcified specimens, than from sections, which only exhibit such parts of it as their plane may happen to traverse. Illustrations from both sources, giving a more complete representation of it than Dr. Dawson's figures afford, have been prepared from the additional specimens placed in my hands.

"It does not appear to me that the canal system takes its origin directly from the cavity of the chambers. On the contrary, I believe that, as in Calcarina (which Dr. Dawson has correctly referred to as presenting the nearest parallel to it

* *Op. cit.*, pp. 50, 51.

among recent Foraminifera), they originate in lacunar spaces on the outside of the proper walls of the chambers, into which the tubuli of those walls open externally; and that the extensions of the sarcode-body which occupied them were formed by the coalescence of the pseudopodia issuing from those tubuli.*

"It seems to me worthy of special notice, that the canal system, wherever displayed in transparent sections, is distinguished by a yellowish brown coloration, so exactly resembling that which I have observed in the canal system of recent Foraminifera (as Polystomella and Calcarina) in which there were remains of the sarcode-body, that I cannot but believe the infiltrating mineral to have been dyed by the remains of sarcode still existing in the canals of Eozoon at the time of its consolidation. If this be the case, the preservation of this colour seems to indicate that no considerable metamorphic action has been exerted upon the rock in which this fossil occurs. And I should draw the same inference from the fact that the organic structure of the shell is in many instances even more completely preserved than it usually is in the Nummulites and other Foraminifera of the Nummulitic limestone of the early Tertiaries.

"To sum up,—That the *Eozoon* finds its proper place in the Foraminiferal series, I conceive to be conclusively proved by its accordance with the great types of that series, in all the essential characters of organization;—namely, the structure of the shell forming the proper wall of the chambers, in which it agrees precisely with Nummulina and its allies; the presence of an intermediate skeleton and an elaborate canal system, the disposition of which reminds us most of Calcarina; a mode of communication of the chambers when they are most completely separated, which has its exact parallel in Cycloclypeus; and an ordinary want of completeness of separation between the chambers, corresponding with that which is characteristic of Carpenteria.

"There is no other group of the animal kingdom to which Eozoon presents the slightest structural resemblance; and to

* *Op. cit.*, p. 221.

the suggestion that it may have been of kin to Nullipore, I can offer the most distinct negative reply, having many years ago carefully studied the structure of that stony Alga, with which that of Eozoon has nothing whatever in common.

"The objections which not unnaturally occur to those familiar with only the ordinary forms of Foraminifera, as to the admission of Eozoon into the series, do not appear to me of any force. These have reference in the first place to the great *size* of the organism; and in the second, to its exceptional mode of growth.

"1. It must be borne in mind that all the Foraminifera normally increase by the continuous gemmation of new segments from those previously formed; and that we have, in the existing types, the greatest diversities in the extent to which this gemmation may proceed. Thus in the Globigerinæ, whose shells cover to an unknown thickness the sea bottom of all that portion of the Atlantic Ocean which is traversed by the Gulf Stream, only eight or ten segments are ordinarily produced by continuous gemmation; and if new segments are developed from the last of these, they detach themselves so as to lay the foundation of independent Globigerinæ. On the other hand in Cycloclypeus, which is a discoidal structure attaining two and a quarter inches in diameter, the number of segments formed by continuous gemmation must be many thousand. Again, the Receptaculites of the Canadian Silurian rocks, shown by Mr. Salter's drawings* to be a gigantic Orbitolite, attains a diameter of twelve inches; and if this were to increase by vertical as well as by horizontal gemmation (after the manner of Tinoporus or Orbitoides) so that one discoidal layer would be piled on another, it would form a mass equalling Eozoon in its ordinary dimensions. To say, therefore, that Eozoon cannot belong to the Foraminifera on account of its gigantic size, is much as if a botanist who had only studied plants and shrubs were to refuse to admit a tree into the same category. The very same continuous gemmation which has produced an Eozoon would produce an equal mass of independent Globigerinæ, if after eight or ten repeti-

* *First Decade of Canadian Fossils*, pl. x.

tions of the process, the new segments were to detach themselves.

"It is to be remembered, moreover, that the largest masses of sponges are formed by continuous gemmation from an original Rhizopod segment; and that there is no *à priori* reason why a Foraminiferal organism should not attain the same dimensions as a Poriferal one,—the intimate relationship of the two groups, notwithstanding the difference between their skeletons, being unquestionable.

"2. The difficulty arising from the zoophytic plan of growth of Eozoon is at once disposed of by the fact that we have in the recent Polytrema (as I have shown, *op. cit.*, p. 235) an organism nearly allied in all essential points of structure to Rotalia, yet no less aberrant in its plan of growth, having been ranked by Lamarck among the Millepores. And it appears to me that Eozoon takes its place quite as naturally in the Nummuline series as Polytrema in the Rotaline. As we are led from the typical Rotalia, through the less regular Planorbulina, to Tinoporus, in which the chambers are piled up vertically, as well as multiplied horizontally, and thence pass by an easy gradation to Polytrema, in which all regularity of external form is lost; so may we pass from the typical Operculina or Nummulina, through Heterostegina and Cycloclypeus to Orbitoides, in which, as in Tinoporus, the chambers multiply both by horizontal and by vertical gemmation; and from Orbitoides to Eozoon the transition is scarcely more abrupt than from Tinoporus to Polytrema.

"The general acceptance, by the most competent judges, of my views respecting the primary value of the characters furnished by the intimate structure of the shell, and the very subordinate value of plan of growth, in the determination of the affinities of Foraminifera, renders it unnecessary that I should dwell further on my reasons for unhesitatingly affirming the Nummuline affinities of Eozoon from the microscopic appearances presented by the proper wall of its chambers, notwithstanding its very aberrant peculiarities; and I cannot but feel it to be a feature of peculiar interest in geological inquiry, that the true relations of by far the earliest fossil yet known should be determinable by the comparison of a portion which the smallest pin's head would cover, with organisms at present existing."

(C.) NOTE ON SPECIMENS FROM LONG LAKE AND WENTWORTH.

[*Journal of Geological Society*, August, 1867.]

"Specimens from Long Lake, in the collection of the Geological Survey of Canada, exhibit white crystalline limestone with light green compact or septariiform* serpentine, and much resemble some of the serpentine limestones of Grenville. Under the microscope the calcareous matter presents a delicate areolated appearance, without lamination; but it is not an example of acervuline Eozoon, but rather of fragments of such a structure, confusedly aggregated together, and having the interstices and cell-cavities filled with serpentine. I have not found in any of these fragments a canal system similar to that of Eozoon Canadense, though there are casts of large stolons, and, under a high power, the calcareous matter shows in many places the peculiar granular or cellular appearance which is one of the characters of the supplemental skeleton of that species. In a few places a tubulated cell-wall is preserved, with structure similar to that of Eozoon Canadense.

"Specimens of Laurentian limestone from Wentworth, in the collection of the Geological Survey, exhibit many rounded silicious bodies, some of which are apparently grains of sand, or small pebbles; but others, especially when freed from the calcareous matter by a dilute acid, appear as rounded bodies, with rough surfaces, either separate or aggregated in lines or groups, and having minute vermicular processes projecting from their surfaces. At first sight these suggest the idea of spicules; but I think it on the whole more likely that they are casts of cavities and tubes belonging to some calcareous Foraminiferal organism which has disappeared. Similar bodies, found in the limestone of Bavaria, have been described by Gümbel, who interprets them in the same way. They may also be com-

* I use the term "septariiform" to denote the *curdled* appearance so often presented by the Laurentian serpentine.

pared with the silicious bodies mentioned in a former paper as occurring in the loganite filling the chambers of specimens of *Eozoon* from Burgess."

These specimens will be more fully referred to under Chapter VI.

(D.) ADDITIONAL STRUCTURAL FACTS.

I may mention here a peculiar and interesting structure which has been detected in one of my specimens while these sheets were passing through the press. It is an abnormal thickening of the calcareous wall, extending across several layers, and perforated with large parallel cylindrical canals, filled with dolomite, and running in the direction of the laminæ; the intervening calcite being traversed by a very fine and delicate canal system. It makes a nearer approach to some of the Stromatoporæ mentioned in Chapter VI. than any other Laurentian structure hitherto observed, and may be either an abnormal growth of Eozoon, consequent on some injury, or a parasitic mass of some Stromatoporoid organism overgrown by the laminæ of the fossil. The structure of the dolomite in this specimen indicates that it first lined the canals, and afterward filled them; an appearance which I have also observed recently in the larger canals filled with serpentine (Plate VIII., fig. 5). The cut below is an attempt, only partially successful, to show the Amœba-like appearance, when magnified, of the casts of the chambers of Eozoon, as seen on the decalcified surface of a specimen broken parallel to the laminæ.

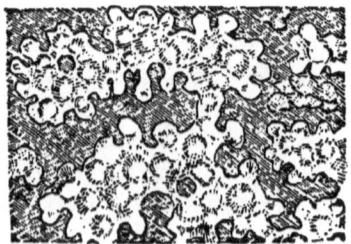

Fig. 21a.

PLATE V.

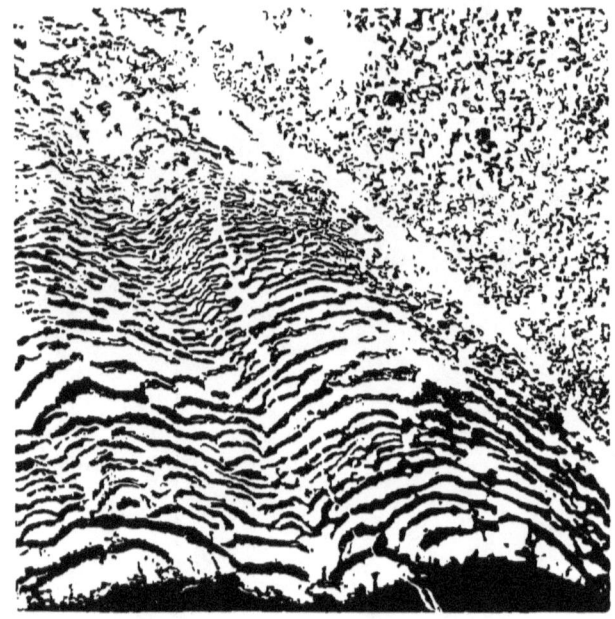

Nature-print of Eozoon, showing laminated, acervuline, and fragmental portions.

This is printed from an electrotype taken from an etched slab of Eozoon, and not touched with a graver except to remedy some accidental flaws in the plate. The diagonal white line marks the course of a calcite vein.

CHAPTER V.

THE PRESERVATION OF EOZOON.

PERHAPS nothing excites more scepticism as to this ancient fossil than the prejudice existing among geologists that no organism can be preserved in rocks so highly metamorphic as those of the Laurentian series. I call this a prejudice, because any one who makes the microscopic structure of rocks and fossils a special study, soon learns that fossils undergo the most remarkable and complete chemical changes without losing their minute structure, and that calcareous rocks if once fossiliferous are hardly ever so much altered as to lose all trace of the organisms which they contained, while it is a most common occurrence to find highly crystalline rocks of this kind abounding in fossils preserved as to their minute structure.

Let us, however, look at the precise conditions under which this takes place.

When calcareous fossils of irregular surface and porous or cellular texture, such as Eozoon was or corals were and are, become imbedded in clay, marl, or other soft sediment, they can be washed out and recovered in a condition similar to that of recent specimens, except that their pores or cells if open may be filled with the material of the matrix, or if not so open that they can be thus filled, they may be more or less incrusted with mineral deposits introduced by water, or may even be completely filled up in this way. But if such fossils are contained in hard rocks, they usually fail, when these are broken, to show their external surfaces, and, breaking across with the containing rock, they exhibit their internal structure merely,—and this more or less distinctly, according to the manner in which their cells or cavities have been filled. Here the microscope becomes of essential service, especially when the structures are minute. A fragment of fossil wood which to the naked eye is nothing but a dark stone, or a coral which is merely a piece of gray or coloured marble, or a specimen of common crystalline limestone made up originally of coral fragments, presents, when sliced and magnified, the most perfect and beautiful structure. In such cases it will be found that ordinarily the original substance of the fossil remains, in a more or less altered state. Wood may be represented by dark lines of coaly matter, or coral by its white or transparent calcareous laminæ; while the material which has been introduced and which fills the cavities may so differ in colour, transparency, or crystalline structure, as to act differently on light, and so reveal the structure. These fillings are very curious. Sometimes they are mere earthy or muddy matter. Sometimes they are pure and transparent and crystalline.

Often they are stained with oxide of iron or coaly matter. They may consist of carbonate of lime, silica or silicates, sulphate of baryta, oxides of iron, carbonate of iron, iron pyrite, or sulphides of copper or lead, all of which are common materials. They are sometimes so complicated that I have seen even the minute cells of woody structures, each with several bands of differently coloured materials deposited in succession, like the coats of an onyx agate.

A further stage of mineralization occurs when the substance of the organism is altogether removed and replaced by foreign matter, either little by little, or by being entirely dissolved or decomposed, leaving a cavity to be filled by infiltration. In this state are some silicified woods, and those corals which have been not filled with but converted into silica, and can thus sometimes be obtained entire and perfect by the solution in an acid of the containing limestone, or by its removal in weathering. In this state are the beautiful silicified corals obtained from the corniferous limestone of Lake Erie. It may be well to present to the eye these different stages of fossilization. I have attempted to do this in fig. 22, taking a tabulate coral of the genus Favosites for an example, and supposing the materials employed to be calcite and silica. Precisely the same illustration would apply to a piece of wood, except that the cell-wall would be carbonaceous matter instead of carbonate of lime. In this figure the dotted parts represent carbonate of lime, the diagonally shaded parts silica or a silicate.

Thus we have, in the natural state, the walls of carbonate of lime and the cavities empty. When fossilized the cavities may be merely filled with carbonate of lime, or they may be filled with silica; or the walls themselves may be replaced by silica and the cavities may remain filled with carbonate of lime; or both the walls and cavities may be represented by or filled with silica or silicates. The ordinary specimens of Eozoon are in the third of these stages, though some

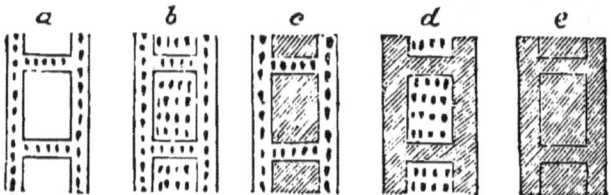

FIG. 22. *Diagram showing different States of Fossilization of a Cell of a Tabulate Coral.*

a.) Natural condition—walls calcite, cell empty. (b.) Walls calcite, cell filled with the same. (c.) Walls calcite, cell filled with silica or silicate. (d.) Walls silicified, cell filled with calcite. (e.) Walls silicified, cell filled with silica or silicate.

exist in the second, and I have reason to believe that some have reached to the fifth. I have not met with any in the fourth stage, though this is not uncommon in Silurian and Devonian fossils.

With regard to the calcareous organisms with which we have now to do, when these are imbedded in pure limestone and filled with the same, so that the whole rock, fossils and all, is identical in composition, and when metamorphic action has caused the whole to become crystalline, and perhaps removed the remains of carbonaceous matter, it may be very difficult to detect any traces of fossils. But even in this case careful management of light may reveal indications of structure, as in some specimens of Eozoon described by the writer and Dr. Carpenter. In many cases, however, even where the limestones have become perfectly crystalline, and the cleavage planes cut freely across the fossils, these exhibit their forms and minute structure in great perfection. This is the case in many of the Lower Silurian limestones of Canada, as I have elsewhere shown.* The gray crystalline Trenton limestone of Montreal, used as a building stone, is an excellent illustration of this. To the naked eye it is a gray marble composed of cleavable crystals; but when examined in thin slices, it shows its organic fragments in the greatest perfection, and all the minute structures are perfectly marked out by delicate carbonaceous lines. The only exception in this limestone is in the case of the Crinoids, in which the cellular structure is filled with transparent calc-spar, perfectly identical with the original solid matter, so that they appear solid and homogeneous, and can be recognised only by their external forms. The specimen represented in fig. 23, is a mass of Corals, Bryozoa, and Crinoids, and shows these under a low power, as represented in the figure; but to the naked eye it is merely a gray crystalline limestone. The specimen represented in fig. 24 shows the Laurentian Eozoon in a similar state of preservation.

* *Canadian Naturalist*, 1859; Microscopic Structure of Canadian Limestones.

It is from a sketch by Dr. Carpenter, and shows the delicate canals partly filled with calcite as clear and

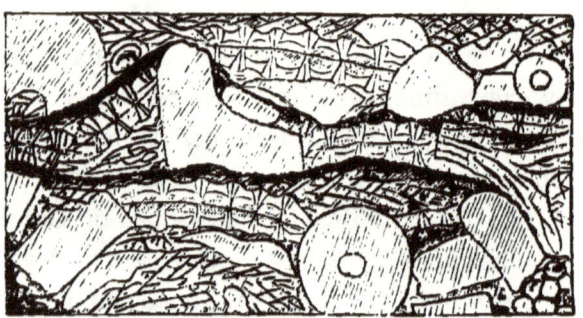

Fig. 23. *Slice of Crystalline Lower Silurian Limestone; showing Crinoids, Bryozoa, and Corals in fragments.*

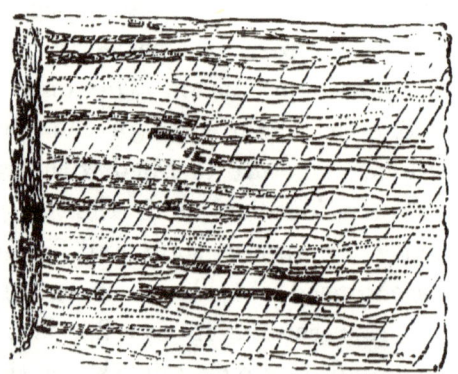

Fig. 24. *Wall of Eozoon penetrated with Canals. The unshaded portions filled with Calcite. (After Carpenter.)*

colourless as that of the shell itself, and distinguishable only by careful management of the light.

In the case of recent and fossil Foraminifers, these —when not so little mineralized that their chambers are empty, or only partially filled, which is sometimes the case even with Eocene Nummulites and Cretaceous forms of smaller size,—are very frequently filled solid with calcareous matter, and as Dr. Carpenter well remarks, even well preserved Tertiary Nummulites in this state often fail greatly in showing their structures, though in the same condition they occasionally show these in great perfection. Among the finest I have seen are specimens from the Mount of Olives (fig. 19), and Dr. Carpenter mentions as equally good those of the London clay of Bracklesham. But in no condition do modern Foraminifera or those of the Tertiary and Mesozoic rocks appear in greater perfection than when filled with the hydrous silicate of iron and potash called glauconite, and which gives by the abundance of its little bottle-green concretions the name of "green-sand" to formations of this age both in Europe and America. In some beds of greensand every grain seems to have been moulded into the interior of a microscopic shell, and has retained its form after the frail envelope has been removed. In some cases the glauconite has not only filled the chambers but has penetrated the fine tubulation, and when the shell is removed, either naturally or by the action of an acid, these project in minute needles or bundles of threads from the surface of the cast. It is in the warmer seas, and especially in the bed of the Ægean and of the Gulf Stream, that such specimens are now most usually found. If we ask why this mineral glauconite should be associated with Foraminiferal shells, the answer is that they are both products of one kind of locality. The same sea bottoms in which Foraminifera most abound are also those in which for some unknown chemical reason glauconite is deposited. Hence no doubt the association of this mineral with the great Foraminiferal formation of the chalk. It is indeed by no means unlikely that the selection by these creatures of the pure carbonate of lime from the sea-water or its minute plants, may be the means of setting free the silica, iron, and potash, in a state suitable for their combination. Similar silicates are found associated with marine limestones, as far back as the Silurian age; and Dr. Sterry Hunt, than whom no one can be a better authority on chemical geology, has argued on chemical grounds that the occurrence of serpentine with the remains of Eozoon is an association of the same character.

However this may be, the infiltration of the pores of Eozoon with serpentine and other silicates has evidently been one main means of the preservation of its structure. When so infiltrated no metamorphism short of the complete fusion of the containing rock could obliterate the minutest points of structure; and that such fusion has not occurred, the preservation in the Laurentian rocks of the most delicate lamination of the beds shows conclusively; while, as already stated, it can be shown that the alteration which has occurred might have taken place at a temperature far short of that necessary to fuse limestone. Thus has it happened that these most ancient fossils have been handed down to our time in a state of preservation comparable, as Dr. Carpenter states, to that of the best preserved fossil Foraminifera from the more recent formations that have come under his observation in the course of all his long experience.

Let us now look more minutely at the nature of the typical specimens of Eozoon as originally observed and described, and then turn to those preserved in other ways, or more or less destroyed and defaced. Taking a polished specimen from Petite Nation, like that delineated in Plate V., we find the shell represented by white limestone, and the chambers by light green serpentine. By acting on the surface with a dilute acid we etch out the calcareous part, leaving a cast in serpentine of the cavities occupied by the soft parts; and when this is done in polished slices these may be made to print their own characters on paper, as has actually been done in the case of Plate V., which is an electrotype taken from an actual specimen, and shows both the laminated and acervuline parts of the fossil. If the process of decalcification has been carefully executed, we find in the excavated spaces delicate ramifying processes of opaque serpentine or transparent dolomite, which were originally imbedded in the calcareous substance, and which are often of extreme fineness and complexity. (Plate VI. and fig. 10.) These are casts of the canals which traversed the shell when still inhabited by the animal. In some well preserved specimens we find the original cell-wall represented by a delicate white film, which under the microscope shows minute needle-like parallel processes representing its still finer tubuli. It is evident that to have filled these tubuli the serpentine must have been introduced in a state of actual solution, and must have carried with it no foreign impurities. Consequently we find that in the chambers themselves the serpentine is pure; and if we examine it under polarized light, we see that it presents a singularly curdled or irregularly laminated appearance, which I have designated under the name septariiform, as if it had an imperfectly crystalline structure, and had been deposited in irregular laminæ, beginning at the sides of the chambers, and filling them toward the middle, and had afterward been cracked by shrinkage, and the cracks filled with a second deposit of serpentine. Now, serpentine is a hydrous silicate of magnesia, and all that we need to suppose is that in the deposits of the Laurentian sea magnesia was present instead of iron and potash, and we can understand that the Laurentian fossil has been petrified by infiltration with serpentine, as more modern Foraminifera have been with glauconite, which, though it usually has little magnesia, often has a considerable percentage of alumina. Further, in specimens of Eozoon from Burgess, the filling mineral is loganite, a compound of silica, alumina, magnesia and iron, with water, and in certain Silurian limestones from New Brunswick and Wales, in which the delicate microscopic pores of the skeletons of stalked star-fishes or Crinoids have been filled with mineral deposits, so that when decalcified these are most beautifully represented by their casts, Dr. Hunt has proved the filling mineral to be a silicate of alumina, iron, magnesia and potash, intermediate between serpentine and glauconite. We have, therefore, ample warrant for adhering to Dr. Hunt's conclusion that the Lauren-

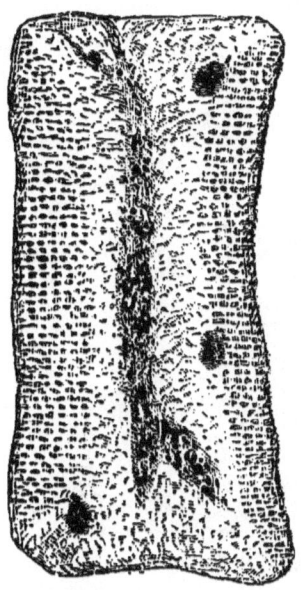

FIG. 25. *Joint of a Crinoid, having its pores injected with a Hydrous Silicate.*
Upper Silurian Limestone, Pole Hill, New Brunswick. Magnified 25 diameters.

tian serpentine was deposited under conditions similar to those of the modern green-sand. Indeed, independently of Eozoon, it is impossible that any geologist who has studied the manner in which this mineral is associated with the Laurentian limestones could believe it to have been formed in any other way. Nor need we be astonished at the fineness of the infiltration by which these minute tubes, perhaps $\frac{1}{10000}$ of an inch in diameter, are filled with mineral matter. The micro-geologist well knows how, in more modern deposits, the finest pores of fossils are filled, and that mineral matter in solution can penetrate the smallest openings that the microscope can detect. Wherever the fluids of the living body can penetrate, there also mineral

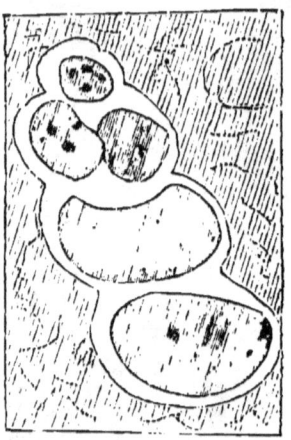

Fig. 26. *Shell from a Silurian Limestone, Wales; its cavity filled with a Hydrous Silicate.*

Magnified 25 diameters.

substances can be carried, and this natural injection, effected under great pressure and with the advantage of ample time, can surpass any of the feats of the anatomical manipulator. Fig. 25 represents a microscopic joint of a Crinoid from the Upper Silurian of New Brunswick, injected with the hydrous silicate already referred to, and fig. 26 shows a microscopic chambered or spiral shell, from a Welsh Silurian limestone, with its cavities filled with a similar substance.

It is only necessary to refer to the attempts which have been made to explain by merely mineral deposits the occurrence of the serpentine in the canals and chambers of Eozoon, and its presenting the form it does, to see that this is the case. Prof. Rowney, for example, to avoid the force of the argument from the canal system, is constrained to imagine that the whole mass has at one time been serpentine, and that this has been partially washed away, and replaced by calcite. If so, whence the deposition of the supposed mass of serpentine, which has to be accounted for in this way as well as in the other? How did it happen to be eroded into so regular chambers, leaving intermediate floors and partitions. And, more wonderful still, how did the regular dendritic bundles, so delicate that they are removed by a breath, remain perfect, and endure until they were imbedded in calcareous spar? Further, how does it happen that in some specimens serpentine and pyroxene seem to have encroached upon the structure, as if they and not calcite were the eroding minerals? How any one who has looked at the structures can for a moment imagine such a possibility, it is difficult to understand. If we could suppose the serpentine to have been originally deposited as a cellular or laminated mass, and its cavities filled with calcite in a gelatinous or semi-fluid state, we might suppose the fine processes of serpentine to have grown outward into these cavities in the mass, as fibres of oxide of iron or manganese have grown in the silica of moss-agate; but this theory would be encompassed with nearly as great mechanical and chemical difficulties. The only rational view that any one can take of the process is, that the calcareous matter was the original substance, and that it had delicate tubes traversing it which became injected with serpentine. The same explanation, and no other, will suffice for those delicate cell-walls, penetrated by innumerable threads of serpentine, which must have been injected into pores. It is true that there are in some of the specimens cracks filled with fibrous serpentine or

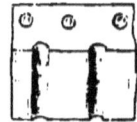 

Fig. 27. *Diagram showing the different appearances of the cell-wall of Eozoon and of a vein of Chrysotile, when highly magnified.*

chrysotile, but these traverse the mass in irregular directions, and they consist of closely packed angular prisms, instead of a matrix of limestone penetrated by cylindrical threads of serpentine. (Fig. 27.) Here I must once for all protest against the tendency of some opponents of Eozoon to confound these structures and the canal system of Eozoon with the acicular crystals, and dendritic or coralloidal forms, observed in some minerals. It is easy to make such comparisons appear plausible to the uninitiated, but practised observers cannot be so deceived, the differences are too marked and essential. In illustration of this, I may refer to the highly magnified canals in figs. 28 and 29. Further, it is evident from the examination of the specimens, that the chrysotile veins, penetrating as they often do

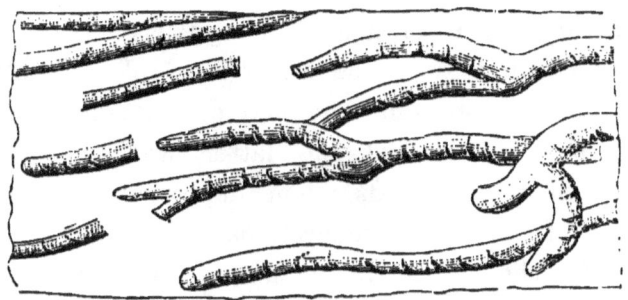

Fig. 23. *Casts of Canals of Eozoon in Serpentine, decalcified and highly magnified.*

Fig. 29. *Canals of Eozoon.*
Highly magnified.

diagonally or transversely across both chambers and walls, must have originated subsequently to the origin and hardening of the rock and its fossils, and result from aqueous deposition of fibrous serpentine in cracks which traverse alike the fossils and their matrix. In specimens now before me, nothing can be more plain than this entire independence of the shining silky veins of fibrous serpentine, and the fact of their having been formed subsequently to the fossilization of the Eozoon; since they can be seen to run across the lamination, and to branch off irregularly in lines altogether distinct from the structure. This, while it shows that these veins have no connection with the fossil, shows also that the latter was an original ingredient of the beds when deposited, and not a product of subsequent concretionary action.

Taking the specimens preserved by serpentine as typical, we now turn to certain other and, in some respects, less characteristic specimens, which are nevertheless very instructive. At the Calumet some of the masses are partly filled with serpentine and partly with white pyroxene, an anhydrous silicate of lime and magnesia. The two minerals can readily be distinguished when viewed with polarized light; and in some slices I have seen part of a chamber or group of canals filled with serpentine and part with pyroxene. In this case the pyroxene or the materials which now compose it, must have been introduced by infiltration, as well as the serpentine. This is the more remarkable as pyroxene is most usually found as an ingredient of igneous rocks; but Dr. Hunt has shown that in the Laurentian limestones and also in veins traversing them, it occurs under conditions which imply its deposition from water, either cold or warm. Gümbel remarks on this:—" Hunt, in a very ingenious manner, compares this formation and deposition of serpentine, pyroxene, and loganite, with that of glauconite, whose formation has gone on uninterruptedly from the Silurian to the Tertiary period, and is even now taking place in the depths of the sea; it being well known that Ehrenberg and others have already shown that many of the grains of glauconite are casts of the interior of foraminiferal shells. In the light of this comparison, the notion that the serpentine and such like minerals of the primitive limestones have been formed, in a similar manner, in the chambers of Eozoic Foraminifera, loses any traces of improbability which it might at first seem to possess."

In many parts of the skeleton of Eozoon, and even in the best infiltrated serpentine specimens, there are portions of the cell-wall and canal system which have been filled with calcareous spar or with dolomite, so similar to the skeleton that it can be detected only under the most favourable lights and with great care. (Fig. 24, *supra*.) The same phenomena may be observed in joints of Crinoids from the Palæozoic rocks, and they constitute proofs of organic origin even more irrefragable than the filling with serpentine. Dr. Carpenter has recently, in replying to the objections of Mr. Carter, made excellent use of this feature of the preservation of Eozoon. It is further to be remarked that in all the specimens of true Eozoon, as well as in many other calcareous fossils preserved in ancient rocks, the calcareous matter, even when its minute structures are not preserved or are obscured, presents a minutely granular or curdled appearance, arising no doubt from the original presence of organic matter, and not recognised in purely inorganic calcite.

Another style of these remarkable fossils is that of the Burgess specimens. In these the walls have been changed into dolomite or magnesian limestone, and the canals seem to have been wholly obliterated, so that only the laminated structure remains. The material filling the chambers is also an aluminous silicate named loganite; and this seems to have been introduced, not so much in solution, as in the state of muddy slime, since it contains foreign bodies, as grains of sand and little groups of silicious concretions, some of which are not unlikely casts of the interior of minute foraminiferal shells contemporary with Eozoon, and will be noticed in the sequel.

Still another mode of occurrence is presented by a remarkable specimen from Tudor in Ontario, and from beds probably on the horizon of the Upper Laurentian or Huronian.* It occurs in a rock scarcely at all metamorphic, and the fossil is represented by white carbonate of lime, while the containing matrix is a dark-coloured coarse limestone. In this specimen the material filling the chambers has not penetrated the canals except in a few places, where they appear filled with dark carbonaceous matter. In mode of preservation these Tudor specimens much resemble the ordinary fossils of the Silurian rocks. One of the specimens in the collection of the Geological Survey

* See Note B, Chap. III.

(fig. 30) presents a clavate form, as if it had been a detached individual supported on one end at the bottom of the sea. It shows, as does also the original Calumet specimen, the septa approaching each other and coalescing at the margin of the form, where there were

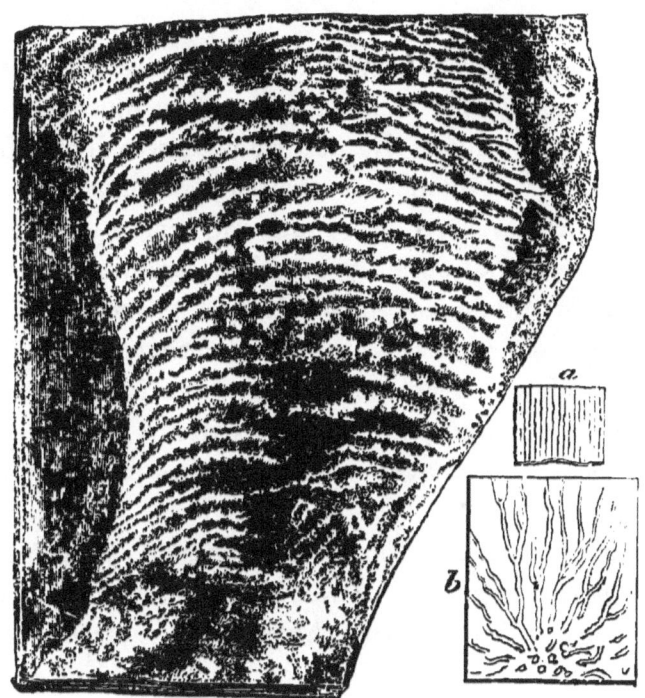

FIG. 30. *Eozoon from Tudor.*
Two-thirds natural size. (*a.*) Tubuli. (*b.*) Canals. Magnified.
a and *b* from another specimen.

probably orifices communicating with the exterior. Other specimens of fragmental Eozoon from the Petite Nation localities have their canals filled with dolomite, which probably penetrated them after they were broken up and imbedded in the rock. I have ascertained with respect to these fragments of Eozoon, that they occur abundantly in certain layers of the Laurentian limestone, beds of some thickness being in great part made up of them, and coarse and fine fragments occur in alternate layers, like the broken corals in some Silurian limestones.

Finally, on this part of the subject, careful observation of many specimens of Laurentian limestone which present no trace of Eozoon when viewed by the naked eye, and no evidence of structure when acted on with acids, are nevertheless organic, and consist of fragments of Eozoon, and possibly of other organisms, not infiltrated with silicates, but only with carbonate of lime, and consequently revealing only obscure indications of their minute structure. I have satisfied myself of this by long and patient investigations, which scarcely admit of any adequate representation, either by words or figures.

Every worker in those applications of the microscope to geological specimens which have been termed microgeology, is familiar with the fact that crystalline forces and mechanical movements of material often play the most fantastic tricks with fossilized organic matter. In fossil woods, for example, we often have the tissues disorganized, with radiating crystallizations of calcite and little spherical concretions of quartz, or disseminated cubes and grains of pyrite, or little veins filled with sulphate of barium or other minerals. We need not, therefore, be surprised to find that in the venerable rocks containing Eozoon, such things occur in the more highly crystalline parts of the limestones, and even in some still showing traces of the fossil. We find many disseminated crystals of magnetite, pyrite, spinel, mica, and other minerals, curiously curved prisms of vermicular mica, bundles of aciculi of tremolite and similar substances, veins of calcite and crysolite or fibrous serpentine, which often traverse the best specimens. Where these occur abundantly we usually find no organic structures remaining, or if they exist they are in a very defective state of preservation. Even in specimens presenting the lamination of Eozoon to the naked eye, these crystalline actions have often destroyed the minute structure; and I fear that some microscopists have been victimised by having under their consideration only specimens in which the actual characters had been too much defaced to be discernible. I must here state that I have found some of the specimens sold under the name of Eozoon Canadense by dealers in microscopical objects to be almost or quite worthless, being destitute of any good structure, and often merely pieces of Laurentian limestone with serpentine grains only. I fear that the circulation of such specimens has done much to cause scepticism as to the Foraminiferal nature of Eozoon. No mistake can be greater than to suppose that any and every specimen of Laurentian limestone must contain Eozoon. More especially have I hitherto failed to detect traces of it in those carbonaceous or graphitic limestones which are so very abundant in the Laurentian country. Perhaps where vegetable matter was very abundant Eozoon did not thrive, or on the other hand the growth of Eozoon may have diminished the quantity of vegetable matter. It is also to be observed that much compression and distortion have occurred in the beds of Laurentian limestone and their contained fossils, and also that the specimens are often broken by faults, some of which are so small as to appear only on microscopic examination, and to shift the plates of the fossil just as if they were beds of rock. This, though it sometimes produces puzzling appearances, is an evidence that the fossils were hard and brittle when this faulting took place, and is consequently an additional proof of their extraneous origin. In some specimens it would seem that the lower and older part of the fossil had been wholly converted into serpentine or pyroxene, or had so nearly experienced this change that only small parts of the calcareous wall can be recognised. These portions correspond with fossil woods altogether silicified, not only by the filling of the cells, but also by the conversion of the walls into silica. I have specimens which manifestly show the transition from the ordinary condition of filling with serpentine to one in which the cell-walls are represented obscurely by one shade of this mineral and the cavities by another.

The above considerations as to mode of preservation of Eozoon concur with those in previous chapters in showing its oceanic character; but the ocean of the Eozoic period may not have been so deep as at present, and its waters were probably warm and well stocked with mineral matters derived from the newly formed land, or from hot springs in its own bottom. On this point the interesting investigations of Dr. Hunt with reference to the chemical conditions of the Silurian seas, allow us to suppose that the Laurentian ocean may have been much more richly stored, more especially with salts of lime and magnesia, than that of subsequent times. Hence the conditions of warmth, light, and nutriment, required by such gigantic Protozoans would all be present, and hence, also no doubt, some of the peculiarities of its mineralization.

NOTES TO CHAPTER V.

(A.) Dr. Sterry Hunt on the Mineralogy of Eozoon and the containing Rocks.

It was fortunate for the recognition of Eozoon that Dr. Hunt had, before its discovery, made so thorough researches into the chemistry of the Laurentian series, and was prepared to show the chemical possibilities of the preservation of fossils in these ancient deposits. The following able summary of his views was appended to the original description of the fossil in the *Journal of the Geological Society*.

"The details of structure have been preserved by the introduction of certain mineral silicates, which have not only filled up the chambers, cells, and canals left vacant by the disappearance of the animal matter, but have in very many cases been injected into the tubuli, filling even their smallest ramifications. These silicates have thus taken the place of the original sarcode, while the calcareous septa remain. It will then be understood that when the replacement of the Eozoon by silicates is spoken of, this is to be understood of the soft parts only; since the calcareous skeleton is preserved, in most cases, without any alteration. The vacant spaces left by the decay of the sarcode may be supposed to have been filled by a process of infiltration, in which the silicates were deposited from solution in water, like the silica which fills up the pores of wood in the process of silicification. The replacing silicates, so far as yet observed, are a white pyroxene, a pale green serpentine, and a dark green alumino-magnesian mineral, which is allied in composition to chlorite and to pyrosclerite, and which I have referred to loganite. The calcareous septa in the last case are found to be dolomitic, but in the other instances are nearly pure carbonate of lime. The relations of the carbonate and the silicates are well seen in thin sections under the microscope, especially by polarized light. The calcite, dolomite, and pyroxene exhibit their crystalline structure to the unaided eye; and the serpentine and loganite are also seen to be crystalline when examined with the microscope. When portions of the fossil are submitted to the action of an acid, the carbonate of lime is dissolved, and a coherent mass of serpentine is obtained, which is a perfect cast of the soft parts of the Eozoon. The form of the sarcode which filled the chambers and cells is beautifully shown, as well as the connecting canals and the groups of tubuli; these latter are seen in great perfection upon surfaces from which the carbonate of lime has been partially dissolved. Their preservation is generally most complete when the replacing mineral is serpentine, although very perfect specimens are sometimes found in pyroxene. The crystallization of the latter mineral appears, however, in most cases to have disturbed the calcareous septa.

"Serpentine and pyroxene are generally associated in these specimens, as if their disposition had marked different stages of a continuous process. At the Calumet, one specimen of the fossil exhibits the whole of the sarcode replaced by serpentine; while, in another one from the same locality, a layer of pale green translucent serpentine occurs in immediate contact with the white pyroxene. The calcareous septa in this specimen are very thin, and are transverse to the plane of contact of the two minerals; yet they are seen to traverse both the pyroxene and the serpentine without any interruption or change. Some sections exhibit these two minerals filling adjacent cells, or even portions of the same cell, a clear line of division being visible between them. In the specimens from Grenville on the other hand, it would seem as if the development of the Eozoon (considerable masses of which were replaced by pyroxene) had been interrupted, and that a second growth of the animal, which was replaced by serpentine, had taken place upon the older masses, filling up their interstices."

[Details of chemical composition are then given.]

"When examined under the microscope, the loganite which replaces the Eozoon of Burgess shows traces of cleavage-lines, which indicate a crystalline structure. The grains of insoluble matter found in the analysis, chiefly of quartz-sand, are distinctly seen as foreign bodies imbedded in the mass, which is moreover marked by lines apparently due to cracks formed by a shrinking of the silicate, and subsequently filled by a further infiltration of the same material. This arrangement resembles on a minute scale that of septaria. Similar appearances are also observed in the serpentine which replaces the Eozoon of Grenville, and also in a massive serpentine from Burgess, resembling this, and enclosing fragments of the fossil. In both of these specimens also grains of mechanical impurities are detected by the microscope; they are however, rarer than in the loganite of Burgess.

"From the above facts it may be concluded that the various silicates which now constitute pyroxene, serpentine, and loganite were directly deposited in waters in the midst of which the Eozoon was still growing, or had only recently perished; and that these silicates penetrated, enclosed, and preserved the calcareous structure precisely as carbonate of lime might have done. The association of the silicates with the Eozoon is only accidental; and large quantities of them, deposited at the same time, include no organic remains. Thus, for example, there are found associated with the Eozoon limestones of Grenville, massive layers and concretions of pure serpentine; and a serpentine from Burgess has already been mentioned as containing only small broken fragments of the fossil. In like manner large masses of white pyroxene, often surrounded by serpentine, both of which are destitute of traces of organic structure, are found in the limestone at the Calumet. In some cases, however, the crystallization of the pyroxene has given rise to considerable cleavage-planes, and has thus obliterated the organic structures from masses which, judging from portions visible here and there, appear to have been at one time penetrated by the calcareous plates of Eozoon. Small irregular veins of crystalline calcite, and of serpentine, are found to traverse such pyroxene masses in the Eozoon limestone of Grenville.

"It appears that great beds of the Laurentian limestones are composed of the ruins of the Eozoon. These rocks, which are white, crystalline, and mingled with pale green serpentine, are similar in aspect to many of the so-called primary limestones of other regions. In most cases the limestones are non-magnesian, but one of them from Grenville was found to be dolomitic. The accompanying strata often present finely crystallized pyroxene, hornblende, phlogopite, apatite, and other minerals. These observations bring the formation of silicious minerals face to face with life, and show that their generation was not incompatible with the contemporaneous existence and the preservation of organic forms. They confirm, moreover, the view which I some years since put forward, that these silicated minerals have been formed, not by subsequent metamorphism in deeply buried sediments, but by reactions going on at the earth's surface.* In support of this view, I have elsewhere referred to the deposition of silicates of lime, magnesia, and iron from natural waters, to the great beds of sepiolite in the unaltered Tertiary strata of Europe; to the contemporaneous formation of neolite (an aluminomagnesian silicate related to loganite and chlorite in composition); and to glauconite, which occurs not only in Secondary, Tertiary, and Recent deposits, but also, as I have shown, in

* *Silliman's Journal* [2], xxix., p. 284; xxxii., p. 286. *Geology of Canada*, p. 577.

Lower Silurian strata.* This hydrous silicate of protoxide of iron and potash, which sometimes includes a considerable proportion of alumina in its composition, has been observed by Ehrenberg, Mantell, and Bailey, associated with organic forms in a manner which seems identical with that in which pyroxene, serpentine, and loganite occur with the Eozoon in the Laurentian limestones. According to the first of these observers, the grains of green-sand, or glauconite, from the Tertiary limestone of Alabama, are casts of the interior of Polythalamia, the glauconite having filled them by 'a species of natural injection, which is often so perfect that not only the large and coarse cells, but also the very finest canals of the cell-walls and all their connecting tubes, are thus petrified and separately exhibited.' Bailey confirmed these observations, and extended them. He found in various Cretaceous and Tertiary limestones of the United States, casts in glauconite, not only of *Foraminifera*, but of spines of *Echinus*, and of the cavities of corals. Besides, there were numerous red, green, and white casts of minute anastomosing tubuli, which, according to Bailey, resemble the casts of the holes made by burrowing sponges (*Cliona*) and worms. These forms are seen after the dissolving of the carbonate of lime by a dilute acid. He found, moreover, similar casts of *Foraminifera*, of minute mollusks, and of branching tubuli, in mud obtained from soundings in the Gulf Stream, and concluded that the deposition of glauconite is still going on in the depths of the sea.† Pourtales has followed up these investigations on the recent formation of glauconite in the Gulf Stream waters. He has observed its deposition also in the cavities of *Millepores*, and in the canals in the shells of *Balanus*. According to him, the glauconite grains formed in *Foraminifera* lose after a time their calcareous envelopes, and finally become 'conglomerated into small black pebbles,' sections of which still show under a microscope the characteristic spiral arrangement of the cells.‡

* *Silliman's Journal* [2], xxxiii., p. 277.   *Geology of Canada*, p. 487.
† *Silliman's Journal* [2], xxii., p. 280.
‡ *Report of United States Coast-Survey*, 1858, p. 248.

"It appears probable from these observations that glauconite is formed by chemical reactions in the ooze at the bottom of the sea, where dissolved silica comes in contact with iron oxide rendered soluble by organic matter; the resulting silicate deposits itself in the cavities of shells and other vacant spaces. A process analagous to this in its results, has filled the chambers and canals of the Laurentian *Foraminifera* with other silicates; from the comparative rarity of mechanical impurities in these silicates, however, it would appear that they were deposited in clear water. Alumina and oxide of iron enter into the composition of loganite as well as of glauconite; but in the other replacing minerals, pyroxene and serpentine, we have only silicates of lime and magnesia, which were probably formed by the direct action of alkaline silicates, either dissolved in surface-waters, or in those of submarine springs, upon the calcareous and magnesian salts of the sea-water."

[As stated in the text, the canals of Eozoon are sometimes filled with dolomite, or in part with serpentine and in part with dolomite.]

(B.) SILURIAN LIMESTONES HOLDING FOSSILS INFILTRATED WITH HYDROUS SILICATE.

Since my attention has been directed to this subject, many illustrations have come under my notice of Silurian limestones in which the pores of fossils are infiltrated with hydrous silicates akin to glauconite and serpentine. A limestone of this kind, collected by Mr. Robb, at Pole Hill, in New Brunswick, afforded not only beautiful specimens of portions of Crinoids preserved in this way, but a sufficient quantity of the material was collected for an exact analysis, a note on which was published in the Proceedings of the Royal Irish Academy, 1871.

The limestone of Pole Hill is composed almost wholly of organic fragments, cemented by crystalline carbonate of lime, and traversed by slender veins of the same mineral. Among the fragments may be recognised under the microscope portions of Trilobites, and of brachiopod and gasteropod shells, and numerous joints and plates of Crinoids. The latter are remarkable for the manner in which their reticulated structure, which is similar to that of modern Crinoids, has been injected with a silicious substance, which is seen distinctly in slices, and still more plainly in decalcified specimens. This filling is precisely similar in appearance to the serpentine filling the canals of Eozoon, the only apparent difference being in the forms of the cells and tubes of the Crinoids, as compared with those of the Laurentian fossil; the same silicious substance also occupies the cavities of some of the small shells, and occurs in mere amorphous pieces, apparently filling interstices. From its mode of occurrence, I have not the slightest doubt that it occupied the cavities of the crinoidal fragments while still recent, and before they had been cemented together by the calcareous paste. This silicious filling is therefore similar on the one hand to that effected by the ancient serpentine of the Laurentian, and on the other to that which results from the depositions of modern glauconite. The analysis of Dr. Hunt, which I give below, fully confirms these analogies.

I may add that I have examined under the microscope portions of the substance prepared by Dr. Hunt for analysis, and find it to retain its form, showing that it is the actual filling of the cavities. I have also examined the small amount of insoluble silica remaining after his treatment with acid and alkaline solvents, and find it to consist of angular and rounded grains of quartzose sand.

The following are Dr. Hunt's notes:—

"The fossiliferous limestone from Pole Hill, New Brunswick, probably of Upper Silurian age, is light gray and coarsely granular. When treated with dilute hydrochloric acid, it leaves a residue of 5·9 per cent., and the solution gives 1·8 per cent. of alumina and oxide of iron, and magnesia equal to 1·35 of carbonate—the remainder being carbonate of lime. The insoluble matter separated by dilute acid, after washing by decantation from a small amount of fine flocculent matter, consists, apart from an admixture of quartz grains, entirely of casts and moulded forms of a peculiar silicate, which Dr. Dawson has observed in decalcified specimens filling the pores of crinoidal stems; and which when separated by an acid, resembles closely under the microscope the corralloidal forms of arragonite known as *flos ferri*, the surfaces being somewhat rugose and glistening with crystalline faces. This silicate is sub-translucent, and of a pale green colour, but immediately becomes of a light reddish brown when heated to redness in the air, and gives off water when heated in a tube, without however, changing its form. It is partially decomposed by strong hydrochloric acid, yielding a considerable amount of protosalt of iron. Strong hot sulphuric acid readily and completely decomposes it, showing it to be a silicate of alumina and ferrous oxide, with some magnesia and alkalies, but with no trace of lime. The separated silica, which remains after the action of the acid, is readily dissolved by a dilute solution of soda, leaving behind nothing but angular and partially rounded grains of sand, chiefly of colourless vitreous quartz. An analysis effected in the way just described on 1·187 grammes gave the following results, which give, by calculation, the centesimal composition of the mineral:—

Silica	·3290	38·93	= 20·77 oxygen.
Alumina	·2440	28·88	= 13·46 ,,
Protoxyd of iron.	·1593	18·86 ⎫	
Magnesia	·0360	4·25 ⎪	= 6·29 ,,
Potash	·0140	1·69 ⎬	
Soda	·0042	·48 ⎭	
Water	·0584	6·91	= 6·14 ,,
Insoluble, quartz	·3420		
	1·1869	100·00	

"A previous analysis of a portion of the mixture by fusion with carbonate of soda gave, by calculation, 18·80 p. c. of protoxide of iron, and amounts of alumina and combined silica closely agreeing with those just given.

"The oxygen ratios, as above calculated, are nearly as 3 : 2 : 1 : 1. This mineral approaches in composition to the jollyte of Von Kobell, from which it differs in containing a portion of alkalies, and only one half as much water. In these respects it agrees nearly with the silicate found by Robert Hoffman, at Raspenau, in Bohemia, where it occurs in thin layers alternating with picrosmine, and surrounding masses of Eozoon in the Laurentian limestones of that region;* the Eozoon itself being there injected with a hydrous silicate which may be described as intermediate between glauconite and chlorite in composition. The mineral first mentioned is compared by Hoffman to fahlunite, to which jollyte is also related in physical characters as well as in composition. Under the names of fahlunite, gigantolite, pinite, etc., are included a great class of hydrous silicates, which from their imperfectly crystalline condition, have generally been regarded, like serpentine, as results of the alteration of other silicates. It is, however, difficult to admit that the silicate found in the condition described by Hoffman, and still more the present mineral, which injects the pores of palæozoic Crinoids, can be any other than an original deposition, allied in the mode of its formation, to the serpentine, pyroxene, and other minerals which have injected the Laurentian Eozoon, and the serpentine and glauconite, which in a similar manner fill Tertiary and recent shells."

(C.) VARIOUS MINERALS FILLING CAVITIES OF FOSSILS IN THE LAURENTIAN.

The following on this subject is from a memoir by Dr. Hunt in the *Twenty-first Report of the Regents of the University of New York*, 1874 :—

"Recent investigations have shown that in some cases the dissemination of certain of these minerals through the crystalline limestones is connected with organic forms. The observations of Dr. Dawson and myself on the Eozoon Canadense showed that certain silicates, namely serpentine, pyroxene, and loganite, had been deposited in the cells and chambers left vacant by the disappearance of the animal matter from the calcareous skeleton of the foraminiferous organism; so that when this calcareous portion is removed by an acid there remains a coherent mass, which is a cast of the soft parts of

* *Journ. für Prakt. Chemie*, Bd. 106 (Erster Jahrgang, 1869), p. 356.

the animal, in which, not only the chambers and connecting canals, but the minute tubuli and pores are represented by solid mineral silicates. It was shown that this process must have taken place immediately after the death of the animal, and must have depended on the deposition of these silicates from the waters of the ocean.

"The train of investigation thus opened up, has been pursued by Dr. Gümbel, Director of the Geological Survey of Bavaria, who, in a recent remarkable memoir presented to the Royal Society of that country, has detailed his results.

"Having first detected a fossil identical with the Canadian Eozoon (together with several other curious microscopic organic forms not yet observed in Canada), replaced by serpentine in a crystalline limestone from the primitive group of Bavaria, which he identified with the Laurentian system of this country, he next discovered a related organism, to which he has given the name of Eozoon Bavaricum. This occurs in a crystalline limestone belonging to a series of rocks more recent than the Laurentian, but older than the Primordial zone of the Lower Silurian, and designated by him the Hercynian clay slate series, which he conceives may represent the Cambrian system of Great Britain, and perhaps correspond to the Huronian series of Canada and the United States. The cast of the soft parts of this new fossil is, according to Gümbel, in part of serpentine, and in part of hornblende.

"His attention was next directed to the green hornblende (pargasite) which occurs in the crystalline limestone of Pargas in Finland, and remains when the carbonate of lime is dissolved as a coherent mass closely resembling that left by the irregular and acervuline forms of Eozoon. The calcite walls also sometimes show casts of tubuli. . . . A white mineral, probably scapolite was found to constitute some tubercles associated with the pargasite, and the two mineral species were in some cases united in the same rounded grain.

"Similar observations were made by him upon specimens of coccolite or green pyroxene, occurring in rounded and wrinkled grains in a Laurentian limestone from New York. These, according to Gümbel, present the same connecting cylinders and branching stems as the pargasite, and are by him supposed to have been moulded in the same manner. . . . Very beautiful evidences of the same organic structure consisting of the casts of tubuli and their ramifications, were also observed by Gümbel in a purely crystalline limestone, enclosing granules of chondrodite, hornblende, and garnet, from Boden in Saxony. Other specimens of limestone, both with and without serpentine and chondrodite, were examined without exhibiting any traces of these peculiar forms; and these negative results are justly deemed by Gümbel as going to prove that the structure of the others is really, like that of Eozoon, the result of the intervention of organic forms. Besides the minerals observed in the replacing substance of Eozoon in Canada, viz., serpentine, pyroxene, and loganite, Gümbel adds chondrodite, hornblende, scapolite, and probably also pyrallolite, quartz, iolite, and dichroite."

(D.) GLAUCONITES.

The following is from a paper by Dr. Hunt in the *Report of the Survey of Canada* for 1866 :—

"In connection with the Eozoon it is interesting to examine more carefully into the nature of the matters which have been called glauconite or green-sand. These names have been given to substances of unlike composition, which, however, occur under similar conditions, and appear to be chemical deposits from water, filling cavities in minute fossils, or forming grains in sedimentary rocks of various ages. Although greenish in colour, and soft and earthy in texture, it will be seen that the various glauconites differ widely in composition. The variety best known, and commonly regarded as the type of the glauconites, is that found in the green-sand of Cretaceous age in New Jersey, and in the Tertiary of Alabama; the glauconite from the Lower Silurian rocks of the Upper Mississippi is identical with it in composition. Analysis shows these glauconites to be essentially hydrous silicates of protoxyd of iron, with more or less alumina, and small but variable quantities of magnesia, besides a notable amount of potash. This alkali is, however, sometimes wanting, as appears from the analysis of a green-sand from Kent in England, by that careful chemist, the late Dr. Edward Turner, and in another examined by Berthier, from the *calcaire grossier*, near Paris, which is essentially a serpentine in composition, being a hydrous silicate of magnesia and protoxyd of iron. A comparison of these last two will show that the loganite, which fills the ancient Foraminifer of Burgess, is a silicate nearly related in composition.

I. Green-sand from the *calcaire grossier*, near Paris. Berthier (cited by Boudant, *Mineralogie*, ii., 178).

II. Green-sand from Kent, England. Dr. Edward Turner (cited by Rogers, Final Report, Geol. N. Jersey, page 206).

III. Loganite from the Eozoon of Burgess.

IV. Green-sand, Lower Silurian; Red Bird, Minnesota.

V. Green-sand, Cretaceous, New Jersey.

VI. Green-sand, Lower Silurian, Orleans Island.

The last four analyses are by myself.

	I.	II.	III.	IV.	V.	VI.
Silica	40·0	48·5	35·14	46·58	50·70	50·7
Protoxyd of iron	24·7	22·0	8·60	20·61	22·50	8·6
Magnesia	16·6	3·8	31·47	1·27	2·16	3·7
Lime	3·3	......	......	2·49	1·11	......
Alumina	1·7	17·0	10·15	11·45	8·03	19·8
Potash	......	traces..	......	6·06	5·80	8·2
Soda	......	......	......	·98	·75	·5
Water	12·6	7·0	14·64	9·66	8·95	8·5
	98·9	98·3	100·00	100·00	100·00	100·0

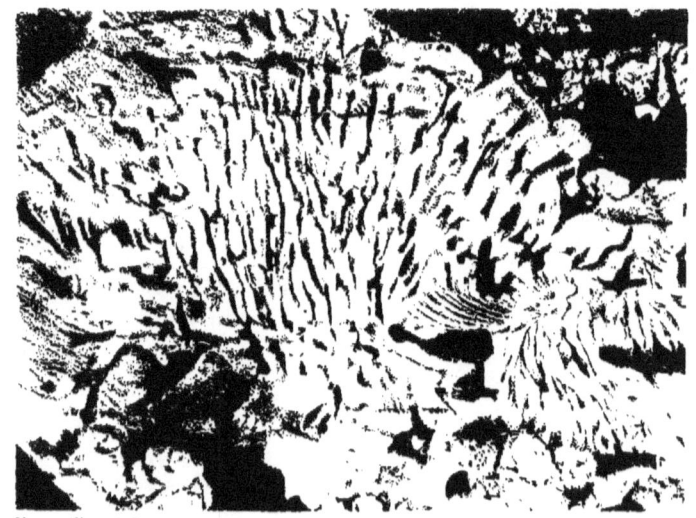

CHAPTER VI.

CONTEMPORARIES AND SUCCESSORS OF EOZOON.

THE name Eozoon, or Dawn-animal, raises the question whether we shall ever know any earlier representative of animal life. Here I think it necessary to explain that in suggesting the name Eozoon for the earliest fossil, and Eozoic for the formation in which it is contained, I had no intention to affirm that there may not have been precursors of the Dawn-animal. By the similar term, Eocene, Lyell did not mean to affirm that there may not have been modern types in the preceding geological periods: and so the dawn of animal life may have had its gray or rosy breaking at a time long anterior to that in which Eozoon built its marble reefs. When the fossils of this early auroral time shall be found, it will not be hard to invent appropriate names for them. There are, however, two reasons that give propriety to the name in the present state of our knowledge. One is, that the Lower Laurentian rocks are absolutely the oldest that have yet come under the notice of geologists, and at the present moment it seems extremely improbable that any older sediments exist, at least in a condition to be recognised as such. The other is that Eozoon, as a member of the group Protozoa, of gigantic size and comprehensive type, and oceanic in its habitat, is as likely as any other creature that can be imagined to have been the first representative of animal life on our planet. Vegetable life may have preceded it, nay probably did so by at least one great creative æon, and may have accumulated previous stores of organic matter; but if any older forms of animal life existed, it is certain at least that they cannot have belonged to much simpler or more comprehensive types. It is also to be observed that such forms of life, if they did exist, may have been naked protozoa, which may have left no sign of their existence except a minute trace of carbonaceous matter, and perhaps not even this.

But if we do not know, and perhaps we are not likely to know, any animals older than Eozoon, may we not find traces of some of its contemporaries, either in the Eozoon limestones themselves, or other rocks associated with them? Here we must admit that a deep sea Foraminiferal limestone may give a very imperfect indication of the fauna of its time. A dredger who should have no other information as to the existing population of the world, except what he could gather from the deposits formed under several hundred fathoms of water, would necessarily have very inadequate conceptions of the matter. In like manner a geologist who should have no other information as to the animal life of the Mesozoic ages than that furnished by some of the thick beds of white chalk might imagine that he had reached a period when the simplest kinds of protozoa predominated over all other forms of life; but this impression would at once be corrected by the examination of other deposits of the same age: so our inferences as to the life of the Laurentian from the contents of its oceanic limestones may be very imperfect, and it may yet yield other and various fossils. Its possibilities are, however, limited by the fact that before we reach this great depth in the earth's crust, we have already left behind in much newer formations all traces of animal life except a few of the lower forms of aquatic invertebrates; so that we are not surprised to find only a limited number of living things, and those of very low type. Do we then know in the Laurentian even a few distinct species, or is our view limited altogether to Eozoon Canadense? In answering this question we must bear in mind that the Laurentian itself was of vast duration, and that important changes of life may have taken place even between the deposition of the Eozoon limestones and that of those rocks in which we find the comparatively rich fauna of the Primordial age. This subject was discussed by the writer as early as 1865, and I may repeat here what could be said in relation to it at that time:—

"In connection with these remarkable remains, it appeared desirable to ascertain, if possible, what share these or other organic structures may have had in the accumulation of the limestones of the Laurentian series. Specimens were therefore selected by Sir W. E. Logan, and slices were prepared under his direction. On microscopic examination, a number of these were found to exhibit merely a granular aggregation of crystals, occasionally with particles of graphite and other foreign minerals, or a laminated mixture of calcareous and other matters, in the manner of some more modern sedimentary limestones. Others, however, were evidently made up almost entirely of fragments of Eozoon, or of mixtures of these with other calcareous and carbonaceous fragments which afford more or less evidence of organic origin. The contents of these organic limestones may be considered under the following heads:—

1. Remains of Eozoon.
2. Other calcareous bodies, probably organic.
3. Objects imbedded in the serpentine.
4. Carbonaceous matters.
5. Perforations, or worm-burrows.

" 1. The more perfect specimens of Eozoon do not constitute the mass of any of the larger specimens in the collection of the Survey; but considerable portions of some of them are made up of material of similar minute structure, destitute of lamination, and irregularly arranged. Some of this material gives the impression that there may have been organisms similar to Eozoon, but growing in an irregular or acervuline manner without lamination. Of this, however, I cannot be certain; and on the other hand there is distinct evidence of the aggregation of fragments of Eozoon in some of these specimens. In some they constitute the greater part of the mass. In others they are embedded in calcareous matter of a different character, or in serpentine or granular pyroxene. In most of the specimens the cells of the fossils are more or less filled with these minerals; and in some instances it would appear that the calcareous matter of fragments of Eozoon has been in part replaced by serpentine."

"2. Intermixed with the fragments of Eozoon above referred to, are other calcareous matters apparently fragmentary. They are of various angular and rounded forms, and present several kinds of structure. The most frequent of these is a strong lamination varying in direction according to the position of the fragments, but corresponding, as far as can be ascertained, with the diagonal of the rhombohedral cleavage. This structure, though crystalline, is highly characteristic of crinoidal remains when preserved in altered limestones. The more dense parts of Eozoon, destitute of tubuli, also sometimes show this structure, though less distinctly. Other fragments are compact and structureless, or show only a fine granular appearance; and these sometimes include grains, patches, or fibres of graphite. In Silurian limestones, fragments of corals and shells which have been partially infiltrated with bituminous matter, show a structure like this. On comparison with altered organic limestones of the Silurian system, these appearances would indicate that in addition to the debris of Eozoon, other calcareous structures, more like those of crinoids, corals, and shells, have contributed to the formation of the Laurentian limestones.

"3. In the serpentine* filling the chambers of a large specimen of Eozoon from Burgess, there are numerous small pieces of foreign matter; and the silicate itself is laminated, indicating its sedimentary nature. Some of the included fragments appear to be carbonaceous, others calcareous; but no distinct organic structure can be detected in them. There are, however, in the serpentine, many minute silicious grains of a bright green colour, resembling greensand concretions; and the manner in which these are occasionally arranged in lines and groups, suggests the supposition that they may possibly be casts of the interior of minute Foraminiferal shells. They may, however, be concretionary in their origin.

"4. In some of the Laurentian limestones submitted to me by Sir W. E. Logan, and in others which I collected some years ago at Madoc, Canada West, there are fibres and granules of carbonaceous matter, which do not conform to the crystalline structure, and present forms quite similar to those which in more modern limestones result from the decomposition of algæ. Though retaining mere traces of organic structure, no doubt would be entertained as to their vegetable origin if they were found in fossiliferous limestones.

"5. A specimen of impure limestone from Madoc, in the collection of the Canadian Geological Survey, which seems from its structure to have been a finely

* This is the dark green mineral named loganite by Dr. Hunt.

laminated sediment, shows perforations of various sizes, somewhat scalloped at the sides, and filled with grains of rounded silicious sand. In my own collection there are specimens of micaceous slate from the same region, with indications on their weathered surfaces of similar rounded perforations, having the aspect of Scolithus, or of worm-burrows.

"Though the abundance and wide distribution of Eozoon, and the important part it seems to have acted in the accumulation of limestone, indicate that it was one of the most prevalent forms of animal existence in the seas of the Laurentian period, the non-existence of other organic beings is not implied. On the contrary, independently of the indications afforded by the limestones themselves, it is evident that in order to the existence and growth of these large Rhizopods, the waters must have swarmed with more minute animal or vegetable organisms on which they could subsist. On the other hand, though this is a less certain inference, the dense calcareous skeleton of Eozoon may indicate that it also was liable to the attacks of animal enemies. It is also possible that the growth of Eozoon, or the deposition of the serpentine and pyroxene in which its remains have been preserved, or both, may have been connected with certain oceanic depths and conditions, and that we have as yet revealed to us the life of only certain stations in the Laurentian seas. Whatever conjectures we may form on these more problematic points, the observations above detailed appear to establish the following conclusions:—

"First, that in the Laurentian period, as in subsequent geological epochs, the Rhizopods were important agents in the accumulation of beds of limestone; and secondly, that in this early period these low forms of animal life attained to a development, in point of magnitude and complexity, unexampled, in so far as yet known, in the succeeding ages of the earth's history. This early culmination of the Rhizopods is in accordance with one of the great laws of the succession of living beings, ascertained from the study of the introduction and progress of other groups; and, should it prove that these great Protozoans were really the dominant type of animals in the Laurentian period, this fact might be regarded as an indication that in these ancient rocks we may actually have the records of the first appearance of animal life on our planet."

With reference to the first of the above heads, I have now to state that it seems quite certain that the upper and younger portions of the masses of Eozoon often passed into the acervuline form, and the period in which this change took place seems to have depended on circumstances. In some specimens there are only a few regular layers, and then a heap of irregular cells. In other cases a hundred or more regular layers were formed; but even in this case little groups of irregular cells occurred at certain points near the surface. This may be seen in plate III. I have also found some masses clearly not fragmental which consist altogether of acervuline cells. A specimen of this kind is represented in fig. 31. It is oval in outline, about three inches in length, wholly made up of rounded or cylindrical cells, the walls of which have a beautiful tubular structure, but there is little or no supplemental skeleton. Whether this is a portion accidentally broken off from the top of a mass of Eozoon, or a peculiar varietal form, or a dis-

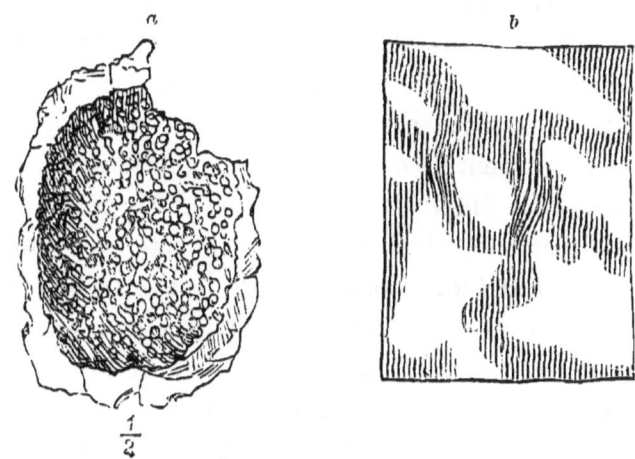

Fig. 31. *Acervuline Variety of Eozoon, St. Pierre.*
(*a.*) General form, half natural size. (*b.*) Portion of cellular interior, magnified, showing the course of the tubuli.

tinct species, it would be difficult to determine. In the meantime I have described it as a variety, "*acervulina*," of the species Eozoon Canadense.* Another variety also, from Petite Nation, shows extremely thin laminæ, closely placed together and very massive, and with little supplemental skeleton. This may be allied to the last, and may be named variety "*minor*."

All this, however, has nothing to do with the layers

* *Proceedings of Geological Society*, 1875.

of fragments of Eozoon which are scattered through the Laurentian limestones. In these the fossil is sometimes preserved in the ordinary manner, with its cavities filled with serpentine, and the thicker parts of the skeleton having their canals filled with this substance. In this case the chambers may have been occupied with serpentine before it was broken up. At St. Pierre there are distinct layers of this kind, from half an inch to several inches in thickness, regularly interstratified with the ordinary limestone. In other layers no serpentine occurs, but the interstices of the fragments are filled with crystalline dolomite or magnesian limestone, which has also penetrated the canals; and there are indications, though less manifest, that some at least of the layers of pure limestone are composed of fragmental Eozoon. In the Laurentian limestone of Wentworth, belonging apparently to the same band with that of St. Pierre, there are many small rounded pieces of limestone, evidently the debris of some older rock, broken up and rounded by attrition. In some of these fragments the structure of Eozoon may be plainly perceived. This shows that still older limestones composed of Eozoon were at that time undergoing waste, and carries our view of the existence of this fossil back to the very beginning of the Laurentian.

With respect to organic fragments not showing the structure of Eozoon, I have not as yet been able to refer these to any definite origin. Some of them may be simply thick portions of the shell of Eozoon with

CONTEMPORARIES AND SUCCESSORS OF EOZOON. 137

their pores filled with calcite, so as to present a homogeneous appearance. Others have much the appearance of fragments of such Primordial forms as *Archæocyathus*, to be described in the sequel; but after much careful search, I have thus far been unable to say more than I could say in 1865.

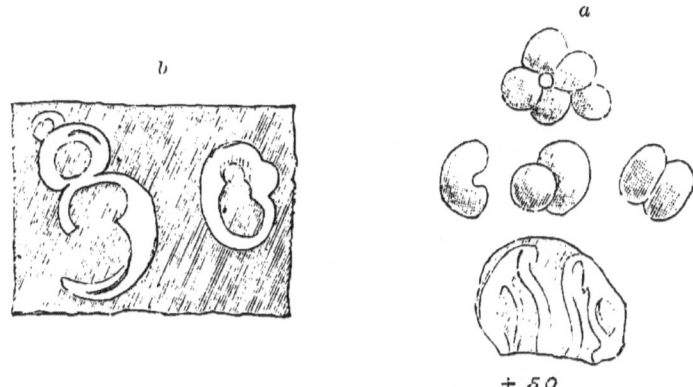

FIG. 32. *Archæospherinæ from St. Pierre.*
(*a.*) Specimens dissolved out by acid. The lower one showing interior septa.
(*b.*) Specimens seen in section.

FIG. 33. *Archæospherinæ from Burgess Eozoon.*
Magnified.

It is different, however, with the round cells infiltrated with serpentine and with the silicious grains included in the loganite. I have already referred to and figured (fig. 18) the remarkable rounded bodies occurring at Long Lake. I now figure similar bodies found mixed with fragmental Eozoon and in separate thin layers at St. Pierre (fig. 32), also some of the singular grains found in the loganite occuping the chambers of Eozoon from Burgess (fig. 33), and a

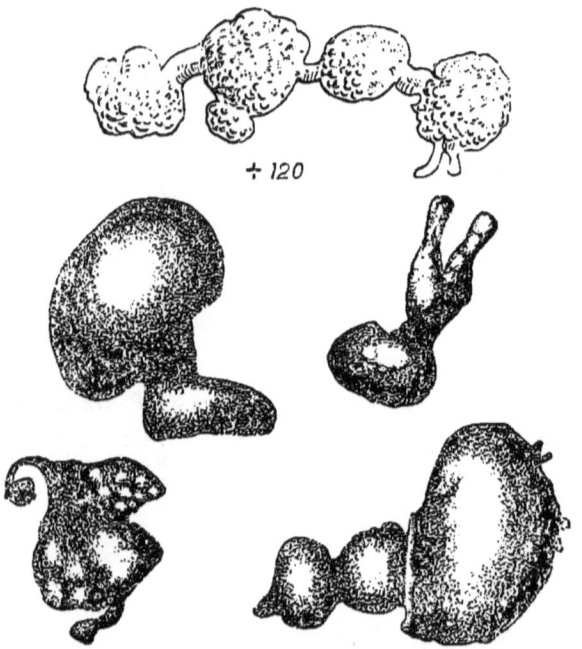

Fig. 34. *Archæospherinæ from Wentworth Limestone.*
Magnified.

beaded body set free by acid, with others of irregular forms, from the limestone of Wentworth (fig. 34). All these I think are essentially of the same nature, namely, chambers originally invested with a tubulated wall like Eozoon, and aggregated in groups, sometimes in a linear manner, sometimes spirally, like those Globigerinæ which constitute the mass of modern deep-sea dredgings and also of the chalk. These bodies occur dispersed in the limestone, arranged in thin layers parallel to the bedding or sometimes in the large chamber-cavities of Eozoon. They are so variable in size and form that it is not unlikely they may be of different origins. The most probable of these may be thus stated. First, they may in some cases be the looser superficial parts of the surface of Eozoon broken up into little groups of cells. Secondly, they may be few-celled germs or buds given off from Eozoon. Thirdly, they may be smaller Foraminifera, structurally allied to Eozoon, but in habit of growth resembling those little globe-shaped forms which, as already stated, abound in chalk and in the modern ocean. The latter view I should regard as highly probable in the case of many of them; and I have proposed for them, in consequence, and as a convenient name, *Archæospherinæ*, or ancient spherical animals.

Carbonaceous matter is rare in the true Eozoon limestones, and, as already stated, I would refer the Laurentian graphite or plumbago mainly to plants. With regard to the worm-burrows referred to in 1865, there can be no doubt of their nature, but there is some doubt as to whether the beds that contain them are really Lower Laurentian. They may be Upper Laurentian or Huronian. I give here figures of these burrows as published in 1866* (fig. 35). The rocks

* *Journal of Geological Society.*

140　THE DAWN OF LIFE.

which contain them hold also fragments of Eozoon, and are not known to contain other fossils.

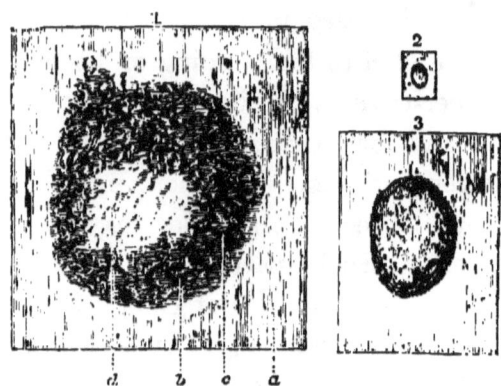

FIG. 35. *Annelid Burrows, Laurentian or Huronian.*

Fig 1. *Transverse section of Worm-burrow*—magnified, as a transparent object. (*a.*) Calcareo-silicious rock. (*b.*) Space filled with calcareous spar. (*c.*) Sand agglutinated and stained black. (*d.*) Sand less agglutinated and uncoloured. Fig. 2. *Transverse section of Worm-burrow on weathered surface*, natural size. Fig. 3. *The same*, magnified.

If we now turn to other countries in search of contemporaries of Eozoon, I may refer first to some specimens found by my friend Dr. Honeyman at Arisaig, in Nova Scotia, in beds underlying the Silurian rocks of that locality, but otherwise of uncertain age. I do not vouch for them as Laurentian, and if of that age they seem to indicate a species distinct from that of Canada proper. They differ in coarser tubulation, and in their canals being large and beaded, and less divergent. I proposed for these specimens, in some notes contributed to the survey of Canada, the name *Eozoon Acadianum*.

Dr. Gumbel, the Director of the Geological Survey

of Bavaria, is one of the most active and widely informed of European geologists, combining European knowledge with an extensive acquaintance with the larger and in some respects more typical areas of the older rocks in America, and stratigraphical geology with enthusiastic interest in the microscopic structures of fossils. He at once and in a most able manner took up the question of the application of the discoveries in Canada to the rocks of Bavaria. The spirit in which he did so may be inferred from the following extract:—

"The discovery of organic remains in the crystalline limestones of the ancient gneiss of Canada, for which we are indebted to the researches of Sir William Logan and his colleagues, and to the careful microscopic investigations of Drs. Dawson and Carpenter, must be regarded as opening a new era in geological science.

"This discovery overturns at once the notions hitherto commonly entertained with regard to the origin of the stratified primary limestones, and their accompanying gneissic and quartzose strata, included under the general name of primitive crystalline schists. It shows us that these crystalline stratified rocks, of the so-called primary system, are only a backward prolongation of the chain of fossiliferous strata; the elements of which were deposited as oceanic sediment, like the clay-slates, limestones, and sandstones of the paleozoic formations, and under similar conditions, though at a time far more remote, and more favourable to the generation of crystalline mineral compounds.

"In this discovery of organic remains in the primary rocks, we hail with joy the dawn of a new epoch in the critical history of these earlier formations. Already in its light, the primeval geological time is seen to be everywhere animated, and peopled with new animal forms of whose very existence we had previously no suspicion. Life, which had hitherto been supposed to have first appeared in the Primordial division of the Silurian period, is now seen to be immeasurably lengthened beyond its former limit, and to embrace in its domain the most ancient known portions of the earth's crust. It would almost seem as if organic life had been awakened simultaneously with the solidification of the earth's crust.

"The great importance of this discovery cannot be clearly understood, unless we first consider the various and conflicting opinions and theories which had hitherto been maintained concerning the origin of these primary rocks. Thus some, who consider them as the first-formed crust of a previously molten globe, regard their apparent stratification as a kind of concentric parallel structure, developed in the progressive cooling of the mass from without. Others, while admitting a similar origin of these rocks, suppose their division into parallel layers to be due, like the lamination of clay-slates, to lateral pressure. If we admit such views, the igneous origin of schistose rocks becomes conceivable, and is in fact maintained by many.

" On the other hand, we have the school which, while recognising the sedimentary origin of these crystalline schists, supposes them to have been metamorphosed at a later period; either by the internal heat, acting in the deeply buried strata; by the proximity of eruptive rocks; or finally, through the agency of permeating waters charged with certain mineral salts.

"A few geologists only have hitherto inclined to the opinion that these crystalline schists, while possessing real stratification, and sedimentary in their origin, were formed at a period when the conditions were more favourable to the production of crystalline materials than at present. According to this view, the crystalline structure of these rocks is an original condition, and not one superinduced at a later period by metamorphosis. In order, however, to arrange and classify these ancient crystalline rocks, it becomes necessary to establish by superposition, or by other evidence, differences in age, such as are recognised in the more recent stratified deposits. The discovery of similar organic remains, occupying a determinate position in the stratification, in different and remote portions of these primitive rocks, furnishes a powerful argument in favour of the latter view, as opposed to the notion which maintains the metamorphic origin of the various minerals and rocks of these ancient formations; so that we may regard the direct formation of these mineral elements, at least so far as these fossiliferous primary limestones are concerned, as an established fact."

His first discovery is thus recorded, in terms which show the very close resemblance of the Bavarian and Canadian Eozoic.

"My discovery of similar organic remains in the serpentine-limestone from near Passau was made in 1865, when I had returned from my geological labours of the summer, and received the recently published descriptions of Messrs. Logan, Dawson, etc. Small portions of this rock, gathered in the progress of the Geological Survey in 1854, and ever since preserved in my collection, having been submitted to microscopic examination, confirmed in the most brilliant manner the acute judgment of the Canadian geologists, and furnished palæontological evidence that, notwithstanding the great distance which separates Canada from Bavaria, the equivalent primitive rocks of the two regions are characterized by similar organic remains; showing at the same time that the law governing the definite succession of organic life on the earth is maintained even in these most ancient formations. The fragments of serpentine-limestone, or ophicalcite, in which I first detected the existence of Eozoon, were like those described in Canada, in which the lamellar structure is wanting, and offer only what Dr. Carpenter has called an acervuline structure. For further confirmation of my observations, I deemed it advisable, through the kindness of Sir Charles Lyell, to submit specimens of the Bavarian rock to the examination of that eminent authority, Dr. Carpenter, who, without any hesitation, declared them to contain Eozoon.

"This fact being established, I procured from the quarries near Passau as many specimens of the limestone as the advanced season of the year would permit; and, aided by my diligent and skilful assistants, Messrs. Reber and Schwager, examined them by the methods indicated by Messrs. Dawson and Carpenter. In this way I soon convinced myself of the general similarity of our organic remains with those of Canada. Our examinations were made on polished sections and in portions etched with dilute nitric acid, or, better, with warm acetic acid. The most beautiful results were however obtained by etching moderately thin sections, so that the specimens may be examined at will either by reflected or transmitted light.

"The specimens in which I first detected Eozoon came from a quarry at Steinhag, near Obernzell, on the Danube, not far from Passau. The crystalline limestone here forms a mass from fifty to seventy feet thick, divided into several beds, included in the gneiss, whose general strike in this region is N.W., with a dip of 40°–60° N.E. The limestone strata of Steinhag have a dip of 45° N.E. The gneiss of this vicinity is chiefly grey, and very silicious, containing dichroite, and of the variety known as dichroite-gneiss; and I conceive it to belong, like the gneiss of Bodenmais and Arber, to that younger division of the primitive gneiss system which I have designated as the Hercynian gneiss formation; which, both to the north, between Tischenreuth and Mahring, and to the south on the north-west of the mountains of Ossa, is immediately overlaid by the mica-slate formation. Lithologically, this newer division of the gneiss is characterized by the predominance of a grey variety, rich in quartz, with black magnesian-mica and orthoclase, besides which a small quantity of oligoclase is never wanting. A further characteristic of this Hercynian gneiss is the frequent intercalation of beds of rocks rich in hornblende, such as hornblende-schist, amphibolite, diorite, syenite, and syenitic granite, and also of serpentine and granulite. Beds of granular limestone, or of calcareous schists are also never altogether wanting; while iron pyrites and graphite, in lenticular masses, or in local beds conformable to the great mass of the gneiss strata, are very generally present.

"In the large quarry of Steinhag, from which I first obtained the Eozoon, the enclosing rock is a grey hornblendic gneiss, which sometimes passes into a hornblende-slate. The limestone is in many places overlaid by a bed of hornblende-schist, sometimes five feet in thickness, which separates it from the normal gneiss. In many localities, a bed of serpentine, three or four feet thick, is interposed between the limestone and the hornblende-schist; and in some cases a zone, consisting chiefly of scapolite, crystalline and almost compact, with an admixture however of hornblende and chlorite. Below the serpentine band, the crystalline limestone appears divided into distinct beds, and encloses various accidental minerals, among which are reddish-white mica, chlorite, hornblende, tremolite, chondrodite, rosellan, garnet, and scapolite, arranged in bands. In several places the lime is mingled with serpentine, grains or portions of which, often of the size of peas, are scattered through the limestone with apparent irregularity, giving rise to a beautiful variety of ophicalcite or serpentine-marble. These portions, which are enclosed in the limestone destitute of serpentine, always present a rounded outline. In one instance there appears, in a high naked wall of limestone without serpentine, the outline of a mass of ophicalcite, about sixteen feet long and twenty-five feet high, which, rising from a broad base, ends in a point, and is separated from the enclosing limestone by an undulating but clearly defined margin, as already well described by Wineberger. This mass of ophicalcite recalls vividly a reef-like structure. Within this and similar masses of ophicalcite in the crystalline limestone, there are, so far as my observations in 1854 extend, no continuous lines or concentric layers of serpentine to be observed, this mineral being always distributed in small grains and patches. The few apparently regular layers which may be observed are soon interrupted, and the whole aggregation is irregular."

It will be observed that this acervuline Eozoon of Steinhag appears to exist in large reefs, and that in its want of lamination it differs from the Canadian examples. In fossils of low organization, like Foraminifera, such differences are often accidental and compatible with specific unity, but yet there may be a difference specifically in the Bavarian Eozoon as compared with the Canadian.

Gümbel also found in the Finnish and Bavarian limestones knotted chambers, like those of Wentworth above mentioned (fig. 36), which he regards as belonging to some other organism than Eozoon; and flocculi having tubes, pores, and reticulations which would seem to point to the presence of structures akin to sponges or possibly remains of seaweeds. These observations Gümbel has extended into other localities in Bavaria and Bohemia, and also in Silesia

Fig. 36. *Archæospherinæ from Pargas in Finland.* (*After Gümbel.*) Magnified.

and Sweden, establishing the existence of Eozoon fossils in all the Laurentian limestones of the middle and north of Europe.

Gümbel has further found in beds overlying the older Eozoic series, and probably of the same age with the Canadian Huronian, a different species of Eozoon, with smaller and more contracted chambers, and still finer and more crowded canals. This, which is to be regarded as a distinct species, or at least a well-marked varietal form, he has named *Eozoon Bavaricum* (fig. 37). Thus this early introduction of life is not peculiar to that old continent which we sometimes call the New

World, but applies to Europe as well, and Europe has furnished a successor to Eozoon in the later Eozoic or Huronian period. In rocks of this age in America, after long search and much slicing of limestones, I have hitherto failed to find any decided organic remains other than the Tudor and Madoc specimens of Eozoon. If these are really Huronian and not Laurentian, the Eozoon from this horizon does not sensibly

Fig. 37. *Section of Eozoon Bavaricum, with Serpentine, from the Crystalline Limestone of the Hercynian primitive Clay-state Formation at Hohenberg; 25 diameters.*

(*a.*) Sparry carbonate of lime. (*b.*) Cellular carbonate of lime. (*c.*) System of tubuli. (*d.*) Serpentine replacing the coarser ordinary variety. (*e.*) Serpentine and hornblende replacing the finer variety, in the very much contorted portions.

differ from that of the Lower Laurentian. The curious limpet-like objects from Newfoundland, discovered by Murray, and described by Billings,* under the name *Aspidella*, are believed to be Huronian, but they have no connection with Eozoon, and therefore need not detain us here.

Leaving the Eozoic age, we find ourselves next in the Primordial or Cambrian, and here we discover the sea

* *Canadian Naturalist*, 1871.

already tenanted by many kinds of crustaceans and shell-fishes, which have been collected and described by palæontologists in Bohemia, Scandinavia, Wales, and North America;* curiously enough, however, the rocks of this age are not so rich in Foraminifera as those of some succeeding periods. Had this primitive type played out its part in the Eozoic and exhausted its energies, and did it remain in abeyance in the Primordial age to resume its activity in the succeeding times? It is not necessary to believe this. The geologist is familiar with the fact, that in one formation he may have before him chiefly oceanic and deep-sea deposits, and in another those of the shallower waters, and that alternations of these may, in the same age or immediately succeeding ages, present very different groups of fossils. Now the rocks and fossils of the Laurentian seem to be oceanic in character, while the Huronian and early Primordial rocks evidence great disturbances, and much coarse and muddy sediment, such as that found in shallows or near the land. They abound in coarse conglomerates, sandstones and thick beds of slate or shale, but are not rich in limestones, which do not in the parts of the world yet explored regain their importance till the succeeding Siluro-Cambrian age. No doubt there were, in the Primordial, deep-sea areas swarming with Foraminifera, the successors of Eozoon; but these are as yet unknown or little known, and our known Primordial fauna is chiefly that of the shallows. Enlarged knowledge may

* Barrande, Angelin, Hicks, Hall, Billings, etc.

thus bridge over much of the apparent gap in the life of these two great periods.

Only as yet on the coast of Labrador and neighbouring parts of North America, and in rocks that were formed in seas that washed the old Laurentian rocks, in which Eozoon was already as fully sealed up as it is at this moment, do we find Protozoa which can claim any near kinship to the proto-foraminifer. These are the fossils of the genus *Archæocyathus*— "ancient cup-sponges, or cup-foraminifers," which have been described in much detail by Mr. Billings in the reports of the Canadian Survey. Mr. Billings regards them as possibly sponges, or as intermediate between these and Foraminifera, and the silicious spicules found in some of them justify this view, unless indeed, as partly suspected by Mr. Billings, these belong to true sponges which may have grown along with Archæocyathus or attached to it. Certain it is, however, that if allied to sponges, they are allied also to Foraminifera, and that some of them deviate altogether from the sponge type and become calcareous chambered bodies, the animals of which can have differed very little from those of the Laurentian Eozoon. It is to these calcareous Foraminiferal species that I shall at present restrict my attention. I give a few figures, for which I am indebted to Mr. Billings, of three of his species (figs. 38 to 40), with enlarged drawings of the structures of one of them which has the most decidedly foraminiferal characters.

To understand Archæocyathus, let us imagine an

inverted cone of carbonate of lime from an inch or two to a foot in length, and with its point buried in the mud at the bottom of the sea, while its open cup

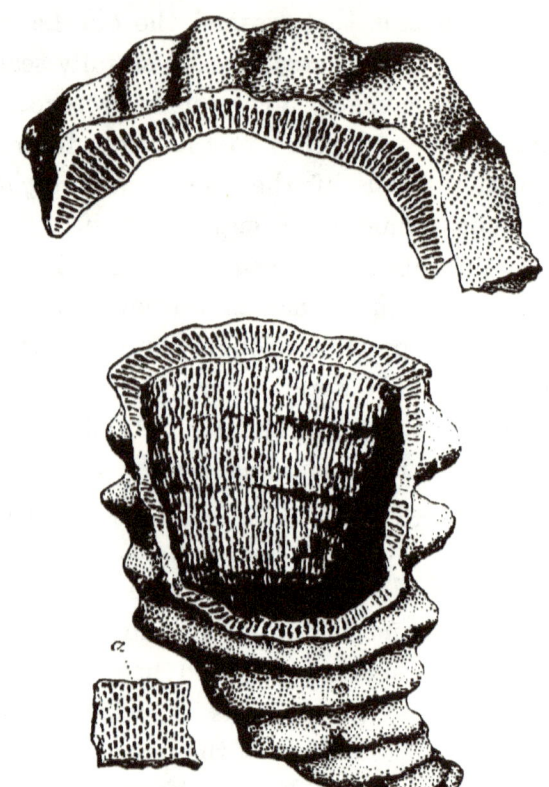

Fig. 38. *Archæocyathus Minganensis—a Primordial Protozoon.*
(*After Billings.*)

(*a.*) Pores of the inner wall.

extends upward into the water. The lower part buried in the soil is composed of an irregular acervuline network of thick calcareous plates, enclosing

Fig. 39. *Archæocyathus profundus—showing the base of attachment and radiating chambers.* (After Billings.)

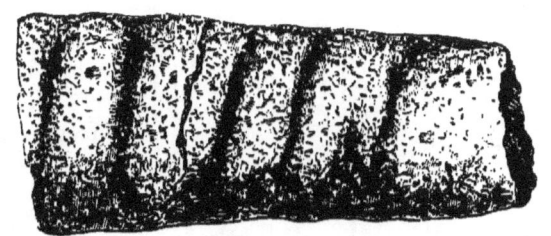

Fig. 40. *Archæocyathus Atlanticus—showing outer surface and longitudinal and transverse sections.* (After Billings.)

chambers communicating with one another (figs. 40 and 41 A). Above this where the cup expands, its walls are composed of thin outer and inner plates, perforated with innumerable holes, and connected with each other by vertical plates, which are also perforated with round pores, establishing a communication between the radiating chambers into which they divide the thickness

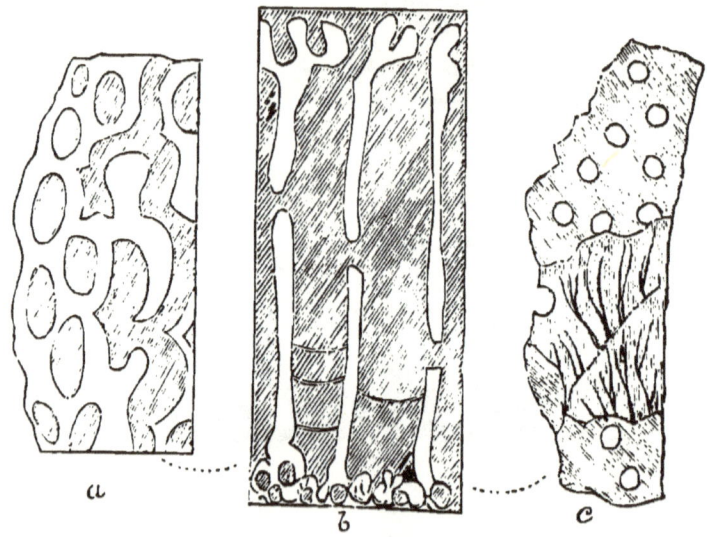

Fig. 41. *Structures of Archæocyathus Profundus.*

(*a.*) Lower acervuline portion. (*b.*) Upper portion, with three of the radiating laminæ. (*c.*) Portion of lamina with pores and thickened part with canals. In figs. *a* and *b* the calcareous part is unshaded.

of the wall (figs. 38, 39, and 41 B). In such a structure the chambers in the wall of the cup and the irregular chambers of the base would be filled with gelatinous animal matter, and the pseudopods would project from the numerous pores in the inner and outer wall. In the older parts of the skeleton, the structure is further complicated by the formation of thin transverse plates, irregular in distribution, and where greater strength is required a calcareous thickening is added, which in some places shows a canal system like that of Eozoon (fig. 41, B, C).* As compared with Eozoon, the fossils want its fine perforated wall, but have a more regular plan of growth. There are fragments in the Eozoon limestones which may have belonged to structures like these; and when we know more of the deep sea of the Primordial, we may recover true species of Eozoon from it, or may find forms intermediate between it and Archæocyathus. In the meantime I know no nearer bond of connection between Eozoon and the Primordial age than that furnished by the ancient cup Zoophytes of Labrador, though I have searched very carefully in the fossiliferous conglomerates of Cambrian age on the Lower St. Lawrence, which contain rocks of all the formations from the Laurentian upwards, often with characteristic fossils. I have also made sections of many of the fossiliferous pebbles in these conglomerates without finding any certain remains of such organisms, though the fragments of the crusts of some of the Primordial tribolites, when their tubuli are infiltrated with dark carbonaceous matter, are so like the supplemental skeleton of Eozoon, that but for

* On the whole these curious fossils, if regarded as Foraminifera, are most nearly allied to the Orbitolites and Dactyloporæ of the Early Tertiary period, as described by Carpenter.

their forms they might readily be mistaken for it; and associated with them are broken pieces of other porous organisms which may belong to Protozoa, though this is not yet certain.

Of all the fossils of the Silurian rocks those which most resemble Eozoon are the *Stromatoporæ*, or "layer-corals," whose resemblance to the old Laurentian fossil at once struck Sir William Logan; and these occur in the earliest great oceanic limestones which succeed the Primordial period, those of the Trenton group, in the Siluro-Cambrian. From this they extend upward as far as the Devonian, appearing everywhere in the limestones, and themselves often constituting large masses of calcareous rock. Our figure (fig. 42) shows a small example of one of these fossils; and when sawn asunder or broken across and weathered, they precisely resemble Eozoon in general appearance, especially when, as sometimes happens, their cell-walls have been silicified.

There are, however, different types of these fossils. The most common, the Stromatoporæ properly so called, consist of concentric layers of calcareous matter attached to each other by pillar-like processes, which, as well as the layers, are made up of little threads of limestone netted together, or radiating from the tops and bottoms of the pillars, and forming a very porous substance. Though they have been regarded as corals by some, they are more generally believed to be Protozoa; but whether more nearly allied to sponges or to Foraminifera may admit of doubt. Some of the more porous kinds are not very dissimilar from calcareous sponges, but they generally want true oscula and pores, and seem better adapted to shield the gelatinous body of a Foraminifer projecting pseudopods in search of food, than that of a sponge, living by the

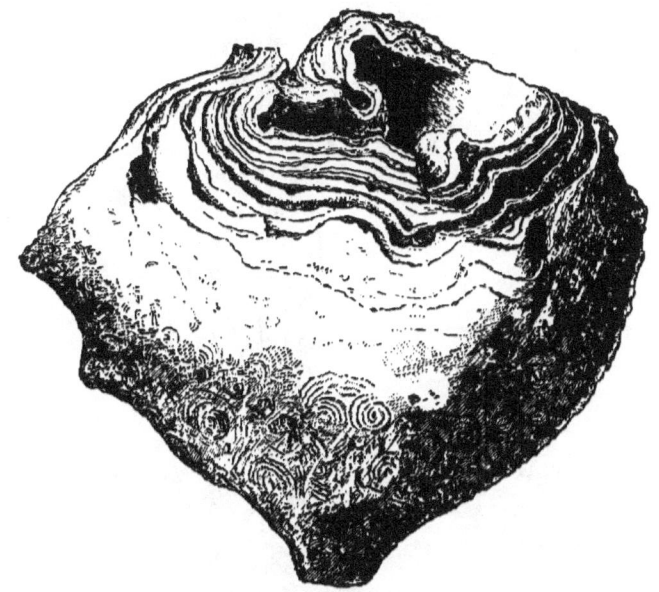

Fig. 42. *Stromatopora rugosa*, Hall—*Lower Silurian, Canada.* (*After Billings.*)

The specimen is of smaller size than usual, and is silicified. It is probably inverted in position, and the concentric marks on the outer surface are due to concretions of silica.

introduction of currents of water. Many of the denser kinds, however, have their calcareous floors so solid that they must be regarded as much more nearly akin to Foraminifers, and some of them have the same irregular inosculation of these floors observed in Eozoon. Figs. 43, A to D, show portions of species of this description, in which the resemblance to Eozoon in structure and arrangement of parts is not remote.

These fossils, however, show no very distinct canal

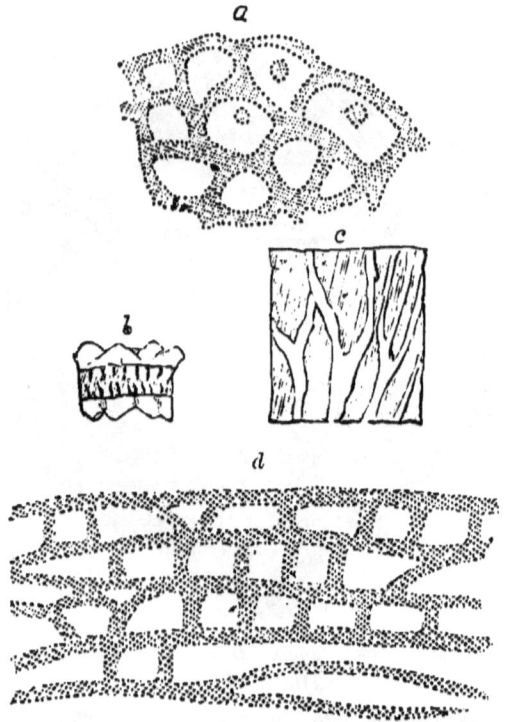

Fig. 43. *Structures of Stromatopora.*

(*a.*) Portion of an oblique section magnified, showing laminæ and columns. (*b.*) Portion of wall with pores, and crusted on both sides with quartz crystals. (*c.*) Thickened portion of wall with canals. (*d.*) Portion of another specimen, showing irregular laminæ and pillars.

system or supplemental skeleton, but this also appears in those forms which have been called Caunopora or Cœnostroma. In these the plates are traversed by tubes, or groups of tubes, which in each successive floor give out radiating and branching canals exactly like those of Eozoon, though more regularly arranged; and if we had specimens with the canals infiltrated with glauconite or serpentine, the resemblance would be perfect. When, as in figs. 44 and 45 A, these canals are seen on the abraded surface, they appear as little grooves arranged in stars, which resemble the radiating plates of corals, but this resemblance is altogether superficial, and I have no doubt that they are really

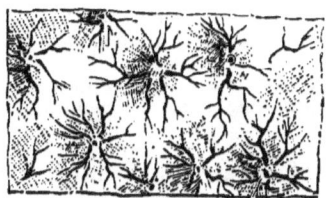

Fig. 44. *Caunopora planulata*, Hall—Devonian; *showing the radiating canals on a weathered surface.* (*After Hall.*)

foraminiferal organisms. This will appear more distinctly from the sections in fig. 45 B, C, which represents an undescribed species recently found by Mr. Weston, in the Upper Silurian limestone of Ontario.

There are probably many species of these curious fossils, but their discrimination is difficult, and their nomenclature confused, so that it would not be profitable to engage the attention of the reader with it except in a note. Their state of preservation, however, is so highly illustrative of that of Eozoon that a word as to this will not be out of place. They are sometimes preserved merely by infiltration with calcite or dolomite, and in this case it is most difficult to make out their minute structures. Often they appear merely as concentrically laminated masses which, but

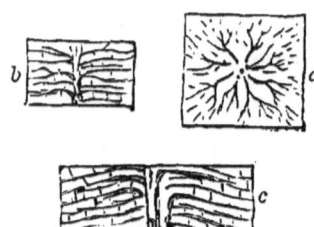

Fig. 45. *Cœnostroma—Guelph Limestone, Upper Silurian, from a specimen collected by Mr. Weston, showing the canals.*

(*a*.) Surface with canals, natural size. (*b*.) Vertical section, natural size. (*c*.) The same magnified, showing canals and laminæ.

for their mode of occurrence, might be regarded as mere concretions. In other cases the cell-walls and pillars are perfectly silicified, and then they form beautiful microscopic objects, especially when decalcified with an acid. In still other cases, they are preserved like Eozoon, the walls being calcareous and the chambers filled with silica. In this state when weathered or decalcified they are remarkably like Eozoon, but I have not met with any having their minute pores and tubes so well preserved as in some of the Laurentian fossils. In many of them, however, the growth and overlapping of the successive amœba-like coats of sarcode can be beautifully seen, exactly as on the surface of a decalcified piece of Eozoon. Those in my collection which most nearly resemble the Laurentian specimens are from the older part of the Lower Silurian series; but unfortunately their minute structures are not well preserved.

In the Silurian and Devonian ages, these Stromatoporæ evidently carried out the same function as the Eozoon in the Laurentian. Winchell tells us that in Michigan and Ohio single specimens can be found several feet in diameter, and that they constitute the mass of considerable beds of limestone. I have myself seen in Canada specimens a foot in diameter, with a great number of laminæ. Lindberg* has given a most vivid account of their occurrence in the Isle of Gothland. He says that they form beds of large irregular discs and balls, attaining a thickness of five Swedish feet, and traceable for miles along the coast, and the individual balls are sometimes a yard in diameter. In some of them the structure is beautifully preserved. In others, or in parts of them, it is reduced to a mass of crystalline limestone. This species is of the Cœnostroma type, and is regarded by Lindberg as a coral, though he admits its low type and resemblance to Protozoa. Its continuous calcareous skeleton he rightly regards as fatal to its claim to be a true sponge. Such a fossil, differing as it does in minute points of structure from Eozoon, is nevertheless probably allied to it in no very distant way, and a successor to its limestone-making function. Those which most nearly approach to Foraminifera are those with thick and solid calcareous laminæ, and with a radiating canal

* *Transactions of Swedish Academy*, 1870.

system; and one of the most Eozoon-like I have seen, is a specimen of the undescribed species already mentioned from the Guelph (Upper Silurian) limestone of Ontario, collected by Mr. Weston, and now in the Museum of the Geological Survey. I have attempted to represent its structures in fig. 44.

In the rocks extending from the Lower Silurian and perhaps from the Upper Cambrian to the Devonian inclusive, the type and function of Eozoon are continued by the Stromatoporæ, and in the earlier part of

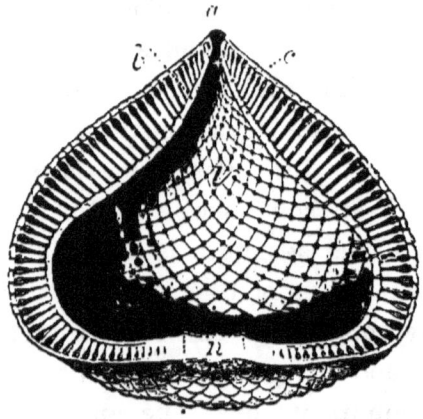

FIG. 46. *Receptaculites, restored.* (*After Billings.*)

(*a.*) Aperture. (*b.*) Inner wall. (*c.*) Outer wall. (*n.*) Nucleus, or primary chamber. (*v.*) Internal cavity.

this time these are accompanied by the Archæocyathids, and by another curious form, more nearly allied to the latter than to Eozoon, the *Receptaculites*. These curious and beautiful fossils, which sometimes are a foot in diameter, consist, like Archæocyathus, of an outer and inner coat enclosing a cavity; but these coats are composed of square plates with pores at the corners, and they are connected by hollow pillars passing in a regular manner from the outer to

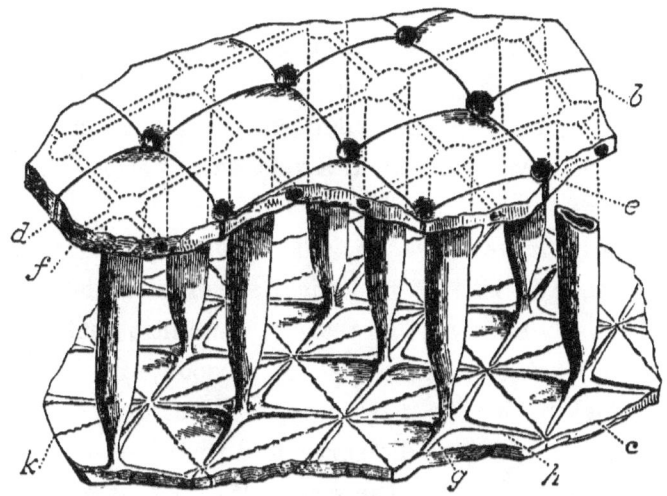

Fig. 47. *Diagram of Wall and Tubes of Receptaculites. (After Billings.)*

(b.) Inner wall. (c.) Outer wall. (d.) Section of plates. (e.) Pore of inner wall. (f.) Canal of inner wall. (g.) Radial stolon. (h.) Cyclical stolon. (k.) Suture of plates of outer wall.

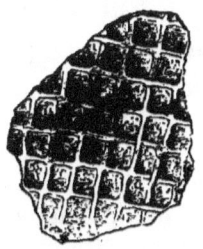

Fig. 48. *Receptaculites, Inner Surface of Outer Wall with the Stolons remaining on its Surface. (After Billings.)*

the inner coat. They have been regarded by Salter as Foraminifers, while Billings considers their nearest analogues to be the seed-like germs of some modern silicious sponges. On the whole, if not Foraminifera, they must have been organisms intermediate between these and sponges, and they certainly constitute one of the most beautiful and complex types of the ancient Protozoa, showing the wonderful perfection to which these creatures attained at a very early period. (Figs. 46, 47, 48.)

I might trace these ancient forms of foraminiferal life further up in the geological series, and show how in the Carboniferous there are nummulitic shells conforming to the general type of Eozoon, and in some cases making up the mass of great limestones.* Further, in the great chalk series and its allied beds, and in the Lower Tertiary, there are not only vast foraminiferal limestones, but gigantic species reminding us of Stromatopora and Eozoon.† Lastly, more diminutive species are doing similar work on a great scale in the modern ocean. Thus we may gather up the broken links of the chain of foraminiferal life, and affirm that Eozoon has never wanted some representative to uphold its family and function throughout all the vast lapse of geological time.

* *Fusulina*, as recently described by Carpenter, *Archæodiscus* of Brady, and the Nummulite recently found in the Carboniferous of Belgium.

† *Parkeria* and *Loftusia* of Carpenter.

NOTE TO CHAPTER VI.

A. STROMATOPORIDÆ, ETC.

For the best description of Archæocyathus, I may refer to *The Palæozoic Fossils of Canada,* by Mr. Billings, vol. i. There also, and in Mr. Salter's memoir in *The Decades of the Canadian Survey,* will be found all that is known of the structure of Receptaculites. For the American Stromatoporæ I may refer to Winchell's paper in the *Proceedings of the American Association,* 1866; to Professor Hall's Descriptions of New Species of Fossils from Iowa, *Report of the State Cabinet, Albany,* 1872; and to the Descriptions of Canadian Species by Dr. Nicholson, in his *Report on the Palæontology of Ontario,* 1874.

The genus Stromatopora of Goldfuss was defined by him as consisting of laminæ of a solid and porous character, alternating and contiguous, and constituting a hemispherical or subglobose mass. In this definition, the porous strata are really those of the fossil, the alternating solid strata being the stony filling of the chambers; and the descriptions of subsequent authors have varied according as, from the state of preservation of the specimens or other circumstances, the original laminæ or the filling of the spaces attracted their attention. In the former case the fossil could be described as consisting of laminæ made up of interlaced fibrils of calcite, radiating from vertical pillars which connect the laminæ. In the latter case, the laminæ appear as solid plates, separated by very narrow spaces, and perforated with round vertical holes representing the connecting pillars. These Stromatoporæ range from the Lower Silurian to the Devonian, inclusive, and many species have been described; but their limits are not very definite, though there are undoubtedly remarkable differences in the distances of the laminæ and in their texture, and in the smooth or mammillated character of the masses. Hall's genus Stromatocerium belongs to these forms, and D'Orbigny's genus Sparsispongia refers to mammillated species, sometimes with apparent oscula.

Phillip's genus Caunopora was formed to receive specimens with concentric cellular layers traversed by "long vermiform cylindrical canals;" while Winchell's genus Cœnostroma includes species with these vermiform canals arranged in a radiate manner, diverging from little eminences in the concentric laminæ. The distinction between these last genera does not seem to be very clear, and may depend on the state of preservation of the specimens. A more important distinction appears to exist between those that have a single vertical canal from which the subordinate canals diverge, and those that have groups of such canals.

Some species of the Cœnostroma group have very dense calcareous laminæ traversed by the canals; but it does not seem that any distinction has yet been made between the proper wall and the intermediate skeleton; and most observers have been prevented from attending to such structures by the prevailing idea that these fossils are either corals or sponges, while the state of preservation of the more delicate tissues is often very imperfect.

B. Localities of Eozoon, or of Limestones supposed to contain it.

In Canada the principal localities of Eozoon Canadense are at Grenville, Petite Nation, the Calumets Rapids, Burgess, Tudor, and Madoc. At the two last places the fossil occurs in beds which may be on a somewhat higher horizon than the others. Mr. Vennor has recently found specimens which have the general form of Eozoon, though the minute structure is not preserved, at Dalhousie, in Lanark Co., Ontario. One specimen from this place is remarkable from having been mineralized in part by a talcose mineral associated with serpentine.

I have examined specimens from Chelmsford, in Massachusetts, and from Amity and Warren County, New York, the latter from the collection of Professor D. S. Martin, which show the canals of Eozoon in a fair state of preservation, though the specimens are fragmental, and do not show the laminated structure.

In European specimens of limestones of Laurentian age, from Tunaberg and Fahlun in Sweden, and from the Western Islands of Scotland, I have hitherto failed to recognise the characteristic structure of the fossil. Connemara specimens have also failed to afford me any satisfactory results, and specimens of a serpentine limestone from the Alps, collected by M. Favre, and communicated to me by Dr. Hunt, though in general texture they much resemble acervuline Eozoon, do not show its minute structures.

PLATE VII.

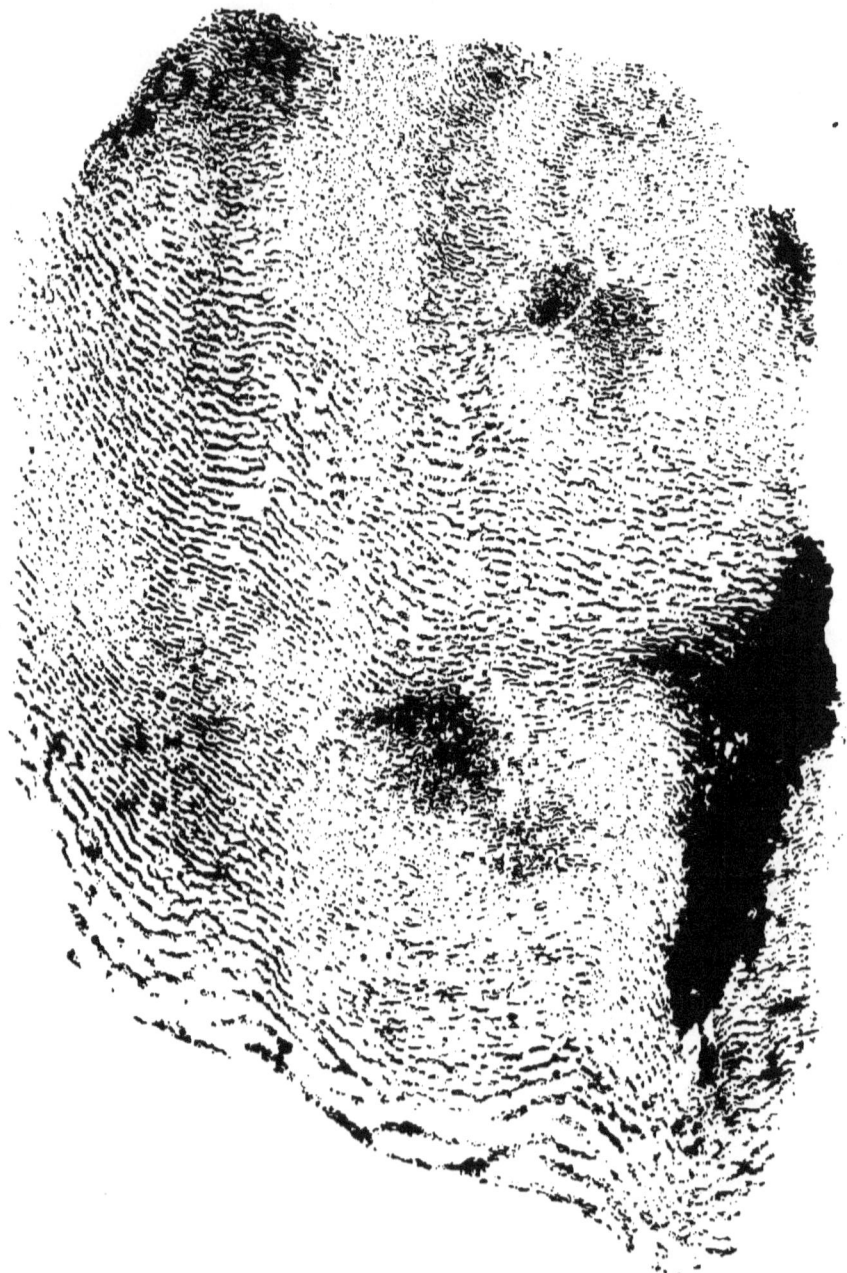

Untouched nature-print of part of a large specimen of Eozoon, from Petite Nation.

The lighter portions are less perfect than in the original, owing to the finer laminæ of serpentine giving way. The dark band at one side is one of the deep lacunæ or oscula.

CHAPTER VII.

OPPONENTS AND OBJECTIONS.

THE active objectors to the animal nature of Eozoon have been few, though some of them have returned to the attack with a pertinacity and determination which would lead one to believe that they think the most sacred interests of science to be dependent on the annihilation of this proto-foraminifer. I do not propose here to treat of the objections in detail. I have presented the case of Eozoon on its own merits, and on these it must stand. I may merely state that the objectors strive to account for the existence of Eozoon by purely mineral deposition, and that the complicated changes which they require to suppose are perhaps the strongest indirect evidence for the necessity of regarding the structures as organic. The reader who desires to appreciate this may consult the notes to this chapter.*

I confess that I feel disposed to treat very tenderly the position of objectors. The facts I have stated make large demands on the faith of the greater part even of naturalists. Very few geologists or naturalists

---

* Also Rowney and King's papers in *Journal Geological Society*, August, 1866; and *Proceedings Irish Academy*, 1870 and 1871.

have much knowledge of the structure of foraminiferal shells, or would be able under the microscope to recognise them with certainty. Nor have they any distinct ideas of the appearances of such structures under different kinds of preservation and mineralisation. Further, they have long been accustomed to regard the so-called Azoic rocks as not only destitute of organic remains, but as being in such a state of metamorphism that these could not have been preserved had they existed. Few, therefore, are able intelligently to decide for themselves, and so they are called on to trust to the investigations of others, and on their testimony to modify in a marked degree their previous beliefs as to the duration of life on our planet. In these circumstances it is rather wonderful that the researches made with reference to Eozoon have met with so general acceptance, and that the resurrection of this ancient inhabitant of the earth has not aroused more of the sceptical tendency of our age.

It must not be lost sight of, however, that in such cases there may exist a large amount of undeveloped and even unconscious scepticism, which shows itself not in active opposition, but merely in quietly ignoring this great discovery, or regarding it with doubt, as an uncertain or unestablished point in science. Such scepticism may best be met by the plain and simple statements in the foregoing chapters, and by the illustrations accompanying them. It may nevertheless be profitable to review some of the points referred to, and to present some considerations making the existence of

Laurentian life less anomalous than may at first sight be supposed. One of these is the fact that the discovery of Eozoon brings the rocks of the Laurentian system into more full harmony with the other geological formations. It explains the origin of the Laurentian limestones in consistency with that of similar rocks in the later periods, and in like manner it helps us to account for the graphite and sulphides and iron ores of these old rocks. It shows us that no time was lost in the introduction of life on the earth. Otherwise there would have been a vast lapse of time in which, while the conditions suitable to life were probably present, no living thing existed to take advantage of these conditions. Further, it gives a more simple beginning of life than that afforded by the more complex fauna of the Primordial age; and this is more in accordance with what we know of the slow and gradual introduction of new forms of living things during the vast periods of Palæozoic time. In connection with this it opens a new and promising field of observation in the older rocks, and if this should prove fertile, its exploration may afford a vast harvest of new forms to the geologists of the present and coming time. This result will be in entire accordance with what has taken place before in the history of geological discovery. It is not very long since the old and semimetamorphic sediments constituting the great Silurian and Cambrian systems were massed together in geological classifications as primitive or primary rocks, destitute or nearly destitute of organic remains. The brilliant discoveries of Sedgwick, Murchison, Barrande, and a host of others, have peopled these once barren regions; and they now stretch before our wondering gaze in the long vistas of early Palæozoic life. So we now look out from the Cambrian shore upon the vast ocean of the Huronian and Laurentian, all to us yet tenantless, except for the few organisms, which, like stray shells cast upon the beach, or a far-off land dimly seen in the distance, incite to further researches, and to the exploration of the unknown treasures that still lie undiscovered. It would be a suitable culmination of the geological work of the last half-century, and one within reach at least of our immediate successors, to fill up this great blank, and to trace back the Primordial life to the stage of Eozoon, and perhaps even beyond this, to predecessors which may have existed at the beginning of the Lower Laurentian, when the earliest sediments of that great formation were laid down. Vast unexplored areas of Laurentian and Huronian rocks exist in the Old World and the New. The most ample facilities for microscopic examination of rocks may now be obtained; and I could wish that one result of the publication of these pages may be to direct the attention of some of the younger and more active geologists to these fields of investigation. It is to be observed also that such regions are among the richest in useful minerals, and there is no reason why search for these fossils should not be connected with other and more practically useful researches. On this subject it will not be out of place to quote the remarks which I made in one of my earlier papers on the Laurentian fossils :—

"This subject opens up several interesting fields of chemical, physiological, and geological inquiry. One of these relates to the conclusions stated by Dr. Hunt as to the probable existence of a large amount of carbonic acid in the Laurentian atmosphere, and of much carbonate of lime in the seas of that period, and the possible relation of this to the abundance of certain low forms of plants and animals. Another is the comparison already instituted by Professor Huxley and Dr. Carpenter, between the conditions of the Laurentian and those of the deeper parts of the modern ocean. Another is the possible occurrence of other forms of animal life than Eozoon and Annelids, which I have stated in my paper of 1864, after extensive microscopic study of the Laurentian limestones, to be indicated by the occurrence of calcareous fragments, differing in structure from Eozoon, but at present of unknown nature. Another is the effort to bridge over, by further discoveries similar to that of the *Eozoon Bavaricum* of Gümbel, the gap now existing between the life of the Lower Laurentian and that of the Primordial Silurian or Cambrian period. It is scarcely too much to say that these inquiries open up a new world of thought and investigation, and hold out the hope of bringing us into the presence of the actual origin of organic life on our planet, though this may perhaps be found to have been Prelaurentian. I would here take the opportunity of stating that, in proposing the name

Eozoon for the first fossil of the Laurentian, and in suggesting for the period the name " Eozoic," I have by no means desired to exclude the possibility of forms of life which may have been precursors of what is now to us the dawn of organic existence. Should remains of still older organisms be found in those rocks now known to us only by pebbles in the Laurentian, these names will at least serve to mark an important stage in geological investigation."

But what if the result of such investigations should be to produce more sceptics, or to bring to light mineral structures so resembling Eozoon as to throw doubt upon the whole of the results detailed in these chapters? I can fancy that this might be the first consequence, more especially if the investigations were in the hands of persons more conversant with minerals than with fossils; but I see no reason to fear the ultimate results. In any case, no doubt, the value of the researches hitherto made may be diminished. It is always the fate of discoverers in Natural Science, either to be followed by opponents who temporarily or permanently impugn or destroy the value of their new facts, or by other investigators who push on the knowledge of facts and principles so far beyond their standpoint that the original discoveries are cast into the shade. This is a fatality incident to the progress of scientific work, from which no man can be free; and in so far as such matters are concerned, we must all be content to share the fate of the old fossils whose history we investigate, and, having served our day and generation to give place to others. If any part of our work should stand the fire of discussion let us be thankful. One thing at least is certain, that such careful surveys as those in the Laurentian rocks of Canada which led to the discovery of Eozoon, and such microscopic examinations as those by which it has been worked up and presented to the public, cannot fail to yield good results of one kind or another. Already the attention excited by the controversies about Eozoon, by attracting investigators to the study of various microscopic and imitative forms in rocks, has promoted the advancement of knowledge, and must do so still more. For my own part, though I am not content to base all my reputation on such work as I have done with respect to this old fossil, I am willing at least to take the responsibility of the results I have announced, whatever conclusions may be finally reached; and in the consciousness of an honest effort to extend the knowledge of nature, to look forward to a better fame than any that could result from the most successful and permanent vindication of every detail of our scientific discoveries, even if they could be pushed to a point which no subsequent investigation in the same difficult line of research would be able to overpass.

Contenting myself with these general remarks, I shall, for the benefit of those who relish geological controversy, append to this chapter a summary of the objections urged by the most active opponents of the animal nature of Eozoon, with the replies that may be or have been given; and I now merely add (in fig. 49) a magnified camera tracing of a portion of a lamina of Eozoon with its canals and tubuli, to show more fully the nature of the structures in controversy.

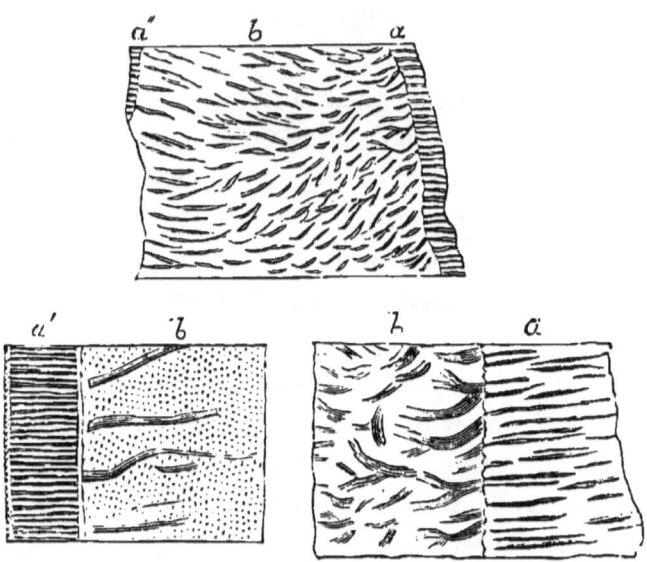

Fig. 49. *Portion of a thin Transverse Slice of a Lamina of Eozoon, magnified, showing its structure, as traced with the camera.*

(a.) Nummuline wall of under side. (b.) Intermediate skeleton with canals. (a'.) Nummuline wall of upper side. The two lower figures show the lower and upper sides more highly magnified. The specimen is one in which the canals are unusually well seen.

It may be well, however, to sum up the evidence as it has been presented by Sir W. E. Logan, Dr. Carpenter, Dr. Hunt, and the author, in a short and intelligible form; and I shall do so under a few brief heads, with some explanatory remarks:—

1. The Lower Laurentian of Canada, a rock forma-

tion whose distribution, age, and structure have been thoroughly worked out by the Canadian Survey, is found to contain thick and widely distributed beds of limestone, related to the other beds in the same way in which limestones occur in the sediments of other geological formations. There also occur in the same formation, graphite, iron ores, and metallic sulphides, in such relations as to suggest the idea that the limestones as well as these other minerals are of organic origin.

2. In the limestones are found laminated bodies of definite form and structure, composed of calcite alternating with serpentine and other minerals. The forms of these bodies suggested a resemblance to the Silurian Stromatoporæ, and the different mineral substances associated with the calcite in the production of similar forms, showed that these were not accidental or concretionary.

3. On microscopic examination, it proved that the calcareous laminæ of these forms were similar in structure to the shells of modern and fossil Foraminifera, more especially those of the Rotaline and Nummuline types, and that the finer structures, though usually filled with serpentine and other hydrous silicates, were sometimes occupied with calcite, pyroxene, or dolomite, showing that they must when recent have been empty canals and tubes.

4. The mode of filling thus suggested for the chambers and tubes of Eozoon, is precisely that which takes place in modern Foraminifera filled with glauconite,

and in Palæozoic crinoids and corals filled with other hydrous silicates.

5. The type of growth and structure predicated of Eozoon from the observed appearances, in its great size, its laminated and acervuline forms, and in its canal system and tubulation, are not only in conformity with those of other Foraminifera, but such as might be expected in a very ancient form of that group.

6. Indications exist of other organic bodies in the limestones containing Eozoon, and also of the Eozoon being preserved not only in reefs but in drifted fragmental beds as in the case of modern corals.

7. Similar organic structures have been found in the Laurentian limestones of Massachusetts and New York, and also in those of various parts of Europe, and Dr. Gümbel has found an additional species in rocks succeeding the Laurentian in age.

8. The manner in which the structures of Eozoon are affected by the faulting, development of crystals, mineral veins, and other effects of disturbance and metamorphism in the containing rocks, is precisely that which might be expected on the supposition that it is of organic origin.

9. The exertions of several active and able opponents have failed to show how, otherwise than by organic agency, such structures as those of Eozoon can be formed, except on the supposition of pseudomorphism and replacement, which must be regarded as chemically extravagant, and which would equally im-

pugn the validity of all fossils determined by microscopic structure. In like manner all comparisons of these structures with dendritic and other imitative forms have signally failed, in the opinion of those best qualified to judge.

Another and perhaps simpler way of putting the case is the following:—Only three general modes of accounting for the existence of Eozoon have been proposed. The first is that of Professors King and Rowney, who regard the chambers and canals filled with serpentine as arising from the erosion or partial dissolving away of serpentine and its replacement by calcite. The objections to this are conclusive. It does not explain the nummuline wall, which has to be separately accounted for by confounding it, contrary to the observed facts, with the veins of fibrous serpentine which actually pass through cracks in the fossil. Such replacement is in the highest degree unlikely on chemical grounds, and there is no evidence of it in the numerous serpentine grains, nodules, and bands in the Laurentian limestones. On the other hand, the opposite replacement, that of limestone by serpentine, seems to have occurred. The mechanical difficulties in accounting for the delicate canals on this theory are also insurmountable. Finally, it does not account for the specimens preserved in pyroxene and other silicates, and in dolomite and calcite. A second mode of accounting for the facts is that the Eozoon forms are merely peculiar concretions. But this fails to account for their great difference from the other serpentine concretions in the same beds, and for their regularity of plan and the delicacy of their structure, and also for minerals of different kinds entering into their composition, and still presenting precisely the same forms and structures. The only remaining theory is that of the filling of cavities by infiltration with serpentine. This accords with the fact that such infiltration by minerals akin to serpentine exists in fossils in later rocks. It also accords with the known aqueous origin of the serpentine nodules and bands, the veins of fibrous serpentine, and the other minerals found filling the cavities of Eozoon. Even the pyroxene has been shown by Hunt to exist in the Laurentian in veins of aqueous origin. The only difficulty existing on this view is how a calcite skeleton with such chambers, canals, and tubuli could be formed; and this is solved by the discovery that all these facts correspond precisely with those to be found in the shells of modern oceanic Foraminifera. The existence then of Eozoon, its structure, and its relations to the containing rocks and minerals being admitted, no rational explanation of its origin seems at present possible other than that advocated in the preceding pages.

If the reader will now turn to Plate VIII., page 207, he will find some interesting illustrations of several very important facts bearing on the above arguments. Fig. 1 represents a portion of a very thin slice of a specimen traversed by veins of fibrous serpentine or chrysotile, and having the calcite of the walls more broken by cleavage planes than usual. The portion selected shows a part of one of the chambers filled with serpentine, which presents the usual curdled aspect almost impossible to represent in a drawing (s). It is traversed by a branching vein of chrysotile (s'), which, where cut precisely parallel to its fibres, shows clear fine cross lines, indicating the sides of its constituent prisms, and where the plane of section has passed obliquely to its fibres, has a curiously stippled or frowsy appearance. On either side of the serpentine band is the nummuline or proper wall, showing under a low power a milky appearance, which, with a higher power, becomes resolved into a tissue of the most beautiful parallel threads, representing the filling of its tubuli. Nothing can be more distinct than the appearances presented by this wall and the chrysotile vein, under every variety of magnifying power and illumination; and all who have had an opportunity of examining my specimens have expressed astonishment that appearances so dissimilar should have been confounded with each other. On the lower side two indentations are seen in the proper wall (c). These are connected with the openings into small subordinate chamberlets, one of which is in part included in the thickness of the slice. At the upper and lower parts of the figure are seen portions of the intermediate skeleton traversed by canals, which in the lower part are very large, though from the analogy of other specimens it is probable that they have in their interstices minute canaliculi not visible in this slice. Fig. 2, from the same specimen, shows the termination of one of the canals against the proper wall, its end expanding into a wide disc of sarcode on the surface of the wall, as may be seen in similar structures in modern Foraminifera. In this specimen the canals are beautifully smooth and cylindrical, but they sometimes present a knotted or jointed appearance, especially in specimens decalcified by acids, in which perhaps some erosion has taken place. They are also occasionally fringed with minute crystals, especially in those specimens in which the calcite has been partially replaced with other minerals. Fig. 3 shows an example of faulting of the proper wall, an appearance not infrequently observed; and it also shows a vein of chrysotile crossing the line of fault, and not itself affected by it—a clear evidence of its posterior origin. Figs. 4 and 5 are examples of specimens having the canals filled with dolomite, and showing extremely fine canals in the interstices of the others: an appearance observed only in the thicker parts of the skeleton, and when these are very well preserved. These dolomitized portions require some precautions for their observation, either in slices or decalcified specimens, but when properly managed they show the structures in very great perfection. The specimen in fig. 5 is from an abnormally thick portion of intermediate skeleton, having unusually thick canals, and referred to in a previous chapter.

One object which I have in view in thus minutely

directing attention to these illustrations, is to show the nature of the misapprehensions which may occur in examining specimens of this kind, and at the same time the certainty which may be attained when proper precautions are taken. I may add that such structures as those referred to are best seen in extremely thin slices, and that the observer must not expect that every specimen will exhibit them equally well. It is only by preparing and examining many specimens that the best results can be obtained. It often happens that one specimen is required to show well one part of the structures, and a different one to show another; and previous to actual trial, it is not easy to say which portion of the structures any particular fragment will show most clearly. This renders it somewhat difficult to supply one's friends with specimens. Really good slices can be prepared only from the best material and by skilled manipulators; imperfect slices may only mislead; and rough specimens may not be properly prepared by persons unaccustomed to the work, or if so prepared may not turn out satisfactory, or may not be skilfully examined. These difficulties, however, Eozoon shares with other specimens in micro-geology, and I have experienced similar disappointments in the case of fossil wood.

In conclusion of this part of the subject, and referring to the notes appended to this chapter for further details, I would express the hope that those who have hitherto opposed the interpretation of Eozoon as organic, and to whose ability and honesty of purpose I willingly bear testimony, will find themselves enabled to acknowledge at least the reasonable probability of that interpretation of these remarkable forms and structures.

NOTES TO CHAPTER VII.

A. OBJECTIONS OF PROFS. KING AND ROWNEY.

Trans. Royal Irish Academy, July, 1869.*

The following summary, given by these authors, may be taken as including the substance of their objections to the animal nature of Eozoon. I shall give them in their words and follow them with short answers to each.

"1st. The serpentine in ophitic rocks has been shown to present appearances which can only be explained on the view that it undergoes structural and chemical changes, causing it to pass into variously subdivided states, and etching out the resulting portions into a variety of forms—grains and plates, with lobulated or segmented surfaces—fibres and aciculi—simple and branching configurations. Crystals of malacolite, often associated with the serpentine, manifest some of these changes in a remarkable degree.

"2nd. The 'intermediate skeleton' of Eozoon (which we hold to be the calcareous matrix of the above lobulated grains, etc.) is completely paralleled in various crystalline rocks—notably marble containing grains of coccolite (Aker and Tyree), pargasite (Finland), chondrodite (New Jersey, etc.).

"3rd. The 'chamber casts' in the acervuline variety of Eozoon are more or less paralleled by the grains of the mineral silicates in the pre-cited marbles.

* Reprinted in the *Annals and Magazine of Natural History*, May, 1874.

"4th. The 'chamber casts' being composed occasionally of loganite and malacolite, besides serpentine, is a fact which, instead of favouring their organic origin, as supposed, must be held as a proof of their having been produced by mineral agencies; inasmuch as these three silicates have a close pseudomorphic relationship, and may therefore replace one another in their naturally prescribed order.

"5th. Dr. Gümbel, observing rounded, cylindrical, or tuberculated grains of coccolite and pargasite in crystalline calcareous marbles, considered them to be 'chamber casts,' or of organic origin. We have shown that such grains often present crystalline planes, angles, and edges; a fact clearly proving that they were originally simple or compound crystals that have undergone external decretion by chemical or solvent action.

"6th. We have adduced evidences to show that the 'nummuline layer' in its typical condition—that is, consisting of cylindrical aciculi, separated by interspaces filled with calcite —has originated directly from closely packed fibres; these from chrysotile or asbestiform serpentine; this from incipiently fibrous serpentine; and the latter from the same mineral in its amorphous or structureless condition.

"7th. The 'nummuline layer,' in its typical condition, unmistakably occurs in cracks or fissures, both in Canadian and Connemara ophite.

"8th. The 'nummuline layer' is paralleled by the fibrous coat which is occasionally present on the surface of grains of chondrodite.

"9th. We have shown that the relative position of two superposed asbestiform layers (an *upper* and an *under* 'proper wall'), and the admitted fact of their component aciculi often passing continuously and without interruption from one 'chamber cast' to another, to the exclusion of the 'intermediate skeleton,' are totally incompatible with the idea of the 'nummuline layer' having resulted from pseudopodial tubulation.

"10th. The so-called 'stolons' and 'passages of communication exactly corresponding with those described in *Cyclo-*

clypeus,' have been shown to be tabular crystals and variously formed bodies, belonging to different minerals, wedged crossways or obliquely in the calcareous interspaces between the grains and plates of serpentine.

"11th. The 'canal system' is composed of serpentine, or malacolite. Its typical kinds in the first of these minerals may be traced in all stages of formation out of plates, prisms, and other solids, undergoing a process of superficial decretion. Those in malacolite are made up of crystals—single, or aggregated together—that have had their planes, angles, and edges rounded off; or have become further reduced by some solvent.

"12th. The 'canal system' in its remarkable branching varieties is completely paralleled by crystalline configurations in the coccolite marble of Aker, in Sweden; and in the crevices of a crystal of spinel imbedded in a calcitic matrix from Amity, New York.

"13th. The *configurations*, presumed to represent the 'canal systems,' are *totally without any regularity* of form, of relative size, or of arrangement; and they occur independently of and apart from other 'eozoonal features' (Amity, Boden, etc.); facts not only demonstrating them to be purely mineral products, but which strike at the root of the idea that they are of organic origin.

"14th. In answer to the argument that as all the foregoing 'eozoonal features' are occasionally found together in ophite, the combination must be considered a conclusive evidence of their organic origin, we have shown, from the composition, physical characters, and circumstances of occurrence and association of their component serpentine, that they represent the structural and chemical changes which are eminently and peculiarly characteristic of this mineral. It has also been shown that the combination is paralleled to a remarkable extent in chondrodite and its calcitic matrix.

"15th. The 'regular alternation of lamellæ of calcareous and silicious minerals' (respectively representing the 'intermediate skeleton' and 'chamber casts') occasionally seen in ophite, and considered to be a 'fundamental fact' evidencing an organic arrangement, is proved to be a *mineralogical* phenomenon by the fact that a similar alternation occurs in amphiboline-calcitic marbles, and gneissose rocks.

"16th. In order to account for certain *untoward* difficulties presented by the configurations forming the 'canal system,' and the aciculi of the 'nummuline layer'—that is, when they occur as '*solid bundles*'—or are '*closely packed*'—or '*appear to be glued together*'—Dr. Carpenter has proposed the theory that the sarcodic extensions which they are presumed to represent have been 'turned into stone' (a 'silicious mineral') 'by Nature's cunning' ('just as the sarcodic layer on the surface of the shell of living Foraminifers is formed by the spreading out of *coalesced* bundles of the pseudopodia that have emerged from the chamber wall')—'by a process of chemical substitution *before* their destruction by ordinary decomposition.' We showed this quasi-alchymical theory to be altogether unscientific.

"17th. The 'silicious mineral' (serpentine) has been analogued with those forming the variously-formed casts (in 'glauconite,' etc.) of recent and fossil Foraminifers. We have shown that the mineral silicates of Eozoon have no relation whatever to the substances composing such casts.

"18th. Dr. Hunt, in order to account for the serpentine, loganite, and malacolite, being the presumed in-filling substances of Eozoon, has conceived the 'novel doctrine,' that such minerals were *directly* deposited in the ocean waters in which this 'fossil' lived. We have gone over all his evidences and arguments without finding *one* to be substantiated.

"19th. Having investigated the alleged cases of 'chambers' and 'tubes' occurring 'filled with calcite,' and presumed to be 'a conclusive answer to' our 'objections,' we have shown that there are the strongest grounds for removing them from the category of reliable evidences on the side of the organic doctrine. The Tudor specimen has been shown to be equally unavailable.

"20th. The occurrence of the best preserved specimens of Eozoon Canadense in rocks that are in a '*highly crystalline condition*' (Dawson) must be accepted as a fact utterly fatal to its organic origin.

"21st. The occurrence of 'eozoonal features' *solely* in crystalline or metamorphosed rocks, belonging to the Laurentian, the Lower Silurian, and the Liassic systems—never in ordinary unaltered deposits of these and the intermediate systems—must be assumed as completely demonstrating their purely mineral origin."

The answers already given to these objections may be summed up severally as follows:—

1st. This is a mere hypothesis to account for the forms presented by serpentine grains and by Eozoon. Hunt has shown that it is untenable chemically, and has completely exploded it in his recent papers on Chemistry and Geology.* My own observations show that it does not accord with the mode of occurrence of serpentine in the Laurentian limestones of Canada.

2nd. Some of the things stated to parallel the intermediate skeleton of Eozoon, are probably themselves examples of that skeleton. Others have been shown to have no resemblance to it.

3rd. The words "more or less" indicate the precise value of this statement, in a question of comparison between mineral and organic structures. So the prismatic structure of satin-spar may be said "more or less" to resemble that of a shell, or of the cells of a Stenopora.

4th. This overlooks the filling of chamber casts with pyroxene, dolomite, or limestone. Even in the case of loganite this objection is of no value unless it can be applied equally to the similar silicates which fill cavities of fossils† in the Silurian limestones and in the greensand.

5th. Dr. Gümbel's observations are those of a highly skilled and accurate observer. Even if crystalline forms appear in "chamber casts," this is as likely to be a result of the injury of organic structures by crystallization, as of the partial effacement of crystals by other actions. Crystalline faces occur abundantly in many undoubted fossil woods and corals; and

---

* Boston, 1874.

† See for a full discussion of this subject Dr. Hunt's "Papers" above referred to.

crystals not unfrequently cross and interfere with the structures in such specimens.

6th. On the contrary, the Canadian specimens prove clearly that the veins of chrysotile have been filled subsequently to the existence of Eozoon in its present state, and that there is no connection whatever between them and the Nummuline wall.

7th. This I have never seen in all my examinations of Eozoon. The writers must have mistaken veins of fibrous serpentine for the nummuline wall.

8th. Only if such grains of chondrodite are themselves casts of foraminiferal chambers. But Messrs. King and Rowney have repeatedly figured mere groups of crystals as examples of the nummuline wall,

9th. Dr. Carpenter has shown that this objection depends on a misconception of the structure of modern Foraminifera, which show similar appearances.

10th. That disseminated crystals occur in the Eozoon limestones is a familiar fact, and one paralleled in many other more or less altered organic limestones. Foreign bodies also occur in the chambers filled with loganite and other minerals; but these need not any more be confounded with the pillars and walls connecting the laminæ than the sand filling a dead coral with its lamellæ. Further, it is well known that foreign bodies are often contained both in the testa and chambers even of recent Foraminifera.

11th. The canal system is not always filled with serpentine or malacolite; and when filled with pyroxene, dolomite, or calcite, the forms are the same. The irregularities spoken of are perhaps more manifest in the serpentine specimens, because this mineral has in places encroached on or partially replaced the calcite walls.

12th. If this is true of the Aker marble, then it must contain Eozoon; and specimens of the Amity limestone which I have examined, certainly contain large fragments of Eozoon.

13th. The configuration of the canal system is quite definite, though varying in coarseness and fineness. It is not known to occur independently of the forms of Eozoon except in fragmental deposits.

14th. The argument is not that they are "occasionally found together in ophite," but that they are found together in specimens preserved by different minerals, and in such a way as to show that all these minerals have filled chambers, canals, and tubuli, previously existing in a skeleton of limestone.

15th. The lamination of Eozoon is not like that of any rock, but a strictly limited and definite form, comparable with that of Stromatopora.

16th. This I pass over, as a mere captious criticism of modes of expression used by Dr. Carpenter.

17th. Dr. Hunt, whose knowledge of chemical geology should give the greatest weight to his judgment, maintains the deposition of serpentine and loganite to have taken place in a manner similar to that of jollyte and glauconite in undoubted fossils: and this would seem to be a clear deduction from the facts he has stated, and from the chemical character of the substances. My own observations of the mode of occurrence of serpentine in the Eozoon limestones lead me to the same result.

18th. Dr. Hunt's arguments on the subject, as recently presented in his *Papers on Chemistry and Geology*, need only be studied by any candid and competent chemist or mineralogist to lead to a very different conclusion from that of the objectors.

19th. This is a mere statement of opinion. The fact remains that the chambers and canals are sometimes filled with calcite.

20th. That the occurrence of Eozoon in crystalline limestones is "utterly fatal" to its claims to organic origin can be held only by those who are utterly ignorant of the frequency with which organic remains are preserved in highly crystalline limestones of all ages. In addition to other examples mentioned above, I may state that the curious specimen of Cœnostroma from the Guelph limestone figured in Chapter VI., has been converted into a perfectly crystalline dolomite, while its canals and cavities have been filled with calcite, since weathered out.

21st. This limited occurrence is an assumption contrary to facts. It leaves out of account the Tudor specimens, and also the abundant occurrence of the Stromatoporoid successors of Eozoon in the Silurian and Devonian. Further, even if the Eozoon were limited to the Laurentian, this would not be remarkable; and since all the Laurentian rocks known to us are more or less altered, it could not in that case occur in unaltered rocks.

I have gone over these objections seriatim, because, though individually weak, they have an imposing appearance in the aggregate, and have been paraded as a conclusive settlement of the questions at issue. They have even been reprinted in the year just past in an English journal of some standing, which professes to accept only original contributions to science, but has deviated from its rule in their favour. I may be excused for adding a portion of my original argument in opposition to these objections, as given more at length in the *Transactions of the Irish Academy*.

1. I object to the authors' mode of stating the question at issue, whereby they convey to the reader the impression that this is merely to account for the occurrence of certain peculiar forms in ophite.

With reference to this, it is to be observed that the attention of Sir William Logan, and of the writer, was first called to Eozoon by the occurrence in Laurentian rocks of definite forms resembling the Silurian *Stromatoporæ*, and dissimilar from any concretions or crystalline structures found in these rocks. With his usual sagacity, Sir William added to these facts the consideration that the mineral substances occurring in these forms were so dissimilar as to suggest that the forms themselves must be due to some extraneous cause rather than to any crystalline or segregative tendency of their constituent minerals. These specimens, which were exhibited by Sir William as probably fossils, at the meeting of the American Association in 1859, and noticed with figures in the Report of the Canadian Survey for 1863, showed under the microscope no minute structures. The writer, who had at the time an opportunity of examining them, stated his belief that if fossils, they would prove to be not Corals but Protozoa.

In 1864, additional specimens having been obtained by the Survey, slices were submitted to the writer, in which he at once detected a well-marked canal-system, and stated, decidedly, his belief that the forms were organic and foraminiferal. The announcement of this discovery was first made by Sir W. E. Logan, in *Silliman's Journal* for 1864. So far, the facts obtained and stated related to definite forms mineralised by loganite, serpentine, pyroxene, dolomite, and calcite. But before publishing these facts in detail, extensive series of sections of all the Laurentian limestones, and of those of the altered Quebec group of the Green Mountain range, were made, under the direction of Sir W. E. Logan and Dr. Hunt, and examined microscopically. Specimens were also decalcified by acids, and subjected to chemical examination by Dr. Sterry Hunt. The result was the conviction that the definite laminated forms must be organic, and further, that there exist in the Laurentian limestones fragments of such forms retaining their structure, and also other fragments, probably organic, but distinct from Eozoon. These conclusions were submitted to the Geological Society of London, in 1864, after the specimens on which they were based had been shown to Dr. Carpenter and Professor T. R. Jones, the former of whom detected in some of the specimens an additional foraminiferal structure—that of the tubulation of the proper wall, which I had not been able to make out. Subsequently, in rocks at Tudor, of somewhat later age than those of the Lower Laurentian at Grenville, similar structures were found in limestones not more metamorphic than many of those which retain fossils in the Silurian system.* I make this historical statement in order to place the question in its true light, and to show that it relates to the organic origin of certain definite mineral masses, exhibiting, not only the external forms of fossils, but also their internal structure.

In opposition to these facts, and to the careful deductions drawn from them, the authors of the paper under consideration maintain that the structures are mineral and crystalline. I believe that in the present state of science such an attempt to return to the doctrine of "plastic-force" as a mode of accounting for fossils would not be tolerated for a moment, were it not for the great antiquity and highly crystalline condition of the rocks in which the structures are found, which naturally create a prejudice against the idea of their being fossiliferous. That the authors themselves feel this is apparent from the slight manner in which they state the leading facts above given, and from their evident anxiety to restrict the question to the mode of occurrence of serpentine in limestone, and to ignore the specimens of Eozoon preserved under different mineral conditions.

2. With reference to the general form of Eozoon and its structure on the large scale, I would call attention to two admissions of the authors of the paper, which appear to me to be fatal to their case:—First, they admit, at page 533 [*Proceedings*, vol. x.], their "inability to explain satisfactorily" the alternating layers of carbonate of lime and other minerals in the typical specimens of Canadian Eozoon. They make a feeble attempt to establish an analogy between this and certain concentric concretionary layers; but the cases are clearly not parallel, and the laminæ of the Canadian Eozoon present connecting plates and columns not explicable on any concretionary hypothesis. If, however, they are unable to explain the lamellar structure alone, as it appeared to Logan in 1859, is it not rash to attempt to explain it away now, when certain minute internal structures, corresponding to what might have been expected on the hypothesis of its organic origin, are added to it? If I affirm that a certain mass is the trunk of a fossil tree, and another asserts that it is a concretion, but professes to be unable to account for its form and its rings of growth, surely his case becomes very weak after I have made a slice of it, and have shown that it retains the structure of wood.

Next, they appear to admit that if specimens occur wholly composed of carbonate of lime, their theory will fall to the ground. Now such specimens do exist. They treat the Tudor specimen with scepticism as probably "strings of segregated calcite." Since the account of that specimen was published, additional fragments have been collected, so that new slices have been prepared. I have examined these with care, and am prepared to affirm that the chambers in these specimens are filled with a dark-coloured limestone not more crystalline than is usual in the Silurian rocks, and that the chamber-walls are composed of carbonate of lime, with the canals filled with the same material, except where the limestone filling the chambers has penetrated into parts of the larger ones. I should add that the stratigraphical researches of Mr. Vennor, of the Canadian Survey, have rendered it probable that the beds containing these fossils, though unconformably underlying the Lower Silurian, overlie the Lower Laurentian of the locality, and are, therefore, probably Upper Laurentian, or perhaps Huronian, so that the Tudor specimens may approach in age to Gümbel's Eozoon Bavaricum.*

Further, the authors of the paper have no right to object to our regarding the laminated specimen as "typical" Eozoon. If the question were as to *typical ophite* the case would be different; but the question actually is as to certain well-defined forms which we regard as fossils, and allege to have organic structure on the small scale, as well as lamination on the large scale. We profess to account for the acervuline forms by the irregular growth at the surface of the organisms, and by the breaking of them into fragments confusedly intermingled in great thicknesses of limestone, just as fragments of corals occur in Palæozoic limestones; but we are under no obligation to accept irregular or disintegrated specimens as typical; and when objectors reason from these fragments, we have a right to point to the more perfect examples. It would be easy to explain the loose cells of *Tetradium* which characterize the bird's-eye limestone of the Lower Silurian of America, as crystalline structures; but a comparison with the unbroken masses of the same coral, shows their true nature. I have for some time made the minute structure of Palæozoic limestones

---

* I may now refer in addition to the canals filled with calcite and dolomite, detected by Dr. Carpenter and myself in specimens from Petite Nation, and mentioned in a previous chapter. See also Plate VIII.

a special study, and have described some of them from the Silurian formations of Canada.* I possess now many additional examples, showing fragments of various kinds of fossils preserved in these limestones, and recognisable only by the infiltration of their pores with different silicious minerals. It can also be shown that in many cases the crystallization of the carbonate of lime, both of the fossils themselves and of their matrix, has not interfered with the perfection of the most minute of these structures.

The fact that the chambers are usually filled with silicates is strangely regarded by the authors as an argument against the organic nature of Eozoon. One would think that the extreme frequency of silicious fillings of the cavities of fossils, and even of silicious replacement of their tissues, should have prevented the use of such an argument, without taking into account the opposite conclusions to be drawn from the various kinds of silicates found in the specimens, and from the modern filling of Foraminifera by hydrous silicates, as shown by Ehrenberg, Mantell, Carpenter, Bailey, and Pourtales.† Further, I have elsewhere shown that the loganite is proved by its texture to have been a fragmental substance, or at least filled with loose *debris;* that the Tudor specimens have the cavities filled with a sedimentary limestone, and that several fragmental specimens from Madoc are actually wholly calcareous. It is to be observed, however, that the wholly calcareous specimens present great difficulties to an observer; and I have no doubt that they are usually overlooked by collectors in consequence of their not being developed by weathering, or showing any obvious structure in fresh fractures.

3. With regard to the canal system, the authors persist in confusing the casts of it which occur in serpentine with "metaxite"· concretions, and in likening them to dendritic crystallizations of silver, etc., and coralloidal forms of carbonate of lime. In answer to this, I think it quite sufficient to say that I fail to perceive the resemblance as other than very

---

* In the *Canadian Naturalist.*
† *Quarterly Journal Geol. Society,* 1864.

imperfectly imitative. I may add, that the case is one of the occurrence of a canal structure in forms which on other grounds appear to be organic, while the concretionary forms referred to are produced under diverse conditions, none of them similar to those of which evidence appears in the specimens of Eozoon. With the singular theory of pseudomorphism, by means of which the authors now supplement their previous objections, I leave Dr. Hunt to deal.

4. With respect to the proper wall and its minute tubulation, the essential error of the authors consists in confounding it with fibrous and acicular crystals, and in maintaining that because the tubuli are sometimes apparently confused and confluent they must be inorganic. With regard to the first of these positions, I may repeat what I have stated in former papers—that the true cell-wall presents minute cylindrical processes traversing carbonate of lime, and usually nearly parallel to each other, and often slightly bulbose at the extremity. Fibrous serpentine, on the other hand, appears as angular crystals, closely packed together, while the numerous spicular crystals of silicious minerals which often appear in metamorphic limestones, and may be developed by decalcification, appear sa sharp angular needles usually radiating from centres or irregularly disposed. Their own plate (Ophite from Skye, King and Rowney's Paper, *Proc. R. I. A.*, vol. x.), is an eminent example of this; and whatever the nature of the crystals represented, they have no appearance of being true tubuli of Eozoon. I have very often shown microscopists and geologists the cell-wall along with veins of chrysotile and coatings of acicular crystals occurring in the same or similar limestones, and they have never failed at once to recognise the difference, especially under high powers.

I do not deny that the tubulation is often imperfectly preserved, and that in such cases the casts of the tubuli may appear to be glued together by concretions of mineral matter, or to be broken or imperfect. But this occurs in all fossils, and is familiar to any microscopist examining them. How difficult is it in many cases to detect the minute structure of Nummulites and other fossil Foraminifera? How often does a specimen of fossil wood present in one part distorted and confused fibres or mere crystals, with the remains of the wood forming phragmata between them, when in other parts it may show the most minute structures in perfect preservation? But who would use the disintegrated portions to invalidate the evidence of the parts better preserved? Yet this is precisely the argument of Professors King and Rowney, and which they have not hesitated in using in the case of a fossil so old as Eozoon, and so often compressed, crushed, and partly destroyed by mineralization.

I have in the above remarks confined myself to what I regard as absolutely essential by way of explanation and defence of the organic nature of Eozoon. It would be unprofitable to enter into the multitude of subordinate points raised by the authors, and their theory of mineral pseudomorphism is discussed by my friend Dr. Hunt; but I must say here that this theory ought, in my opinion, to afford to any chemist a strong presumption against the validity of their objections, especially since it confessedly does not account for all the facts, while requiring a most complicated series of unproved and improbable suppositions.

The only other new features in the communication to which this note refers are contained in the "supplementary note." The first of these relates to the grains of coccolite in the limestone of Aker, in Sweden. Whether or not these are organic, they are apparently different from *Eozoon Canadense*. They, no doubt, resemble the grains referred to by Gümbel as possibly organic, and also similar granular objects with projections which, in a previous paper, I have described from Laurentian limestones in Canada. These objects are of doubtful nature; but if organic, they are distinct from Eozoon. The second relates to the supposed crystals of malacolite from the same place. Admitting the interpretation given of these to be correct, they are no more related to Eozoon than are the curious vermicular crystals of a micaceous mineral which I have noticed in the Canadian limestones.

The third and still more remarkable case is that of a spinel from Amity, New York, containing calcite in its crevices, including a perfect canal system preserved in malacolite. With reference to this, as spinels of large size occur in veins in the Laurentian rocks, I am not prepared to say that it is absolutely impossible that fragments of limestone containing Eozoon may not be occasionally associated with them in their matrix. I confess, however, that until I can examine such specimens, which I have not yet met with, I cannot, after my experience of the tendencies of Messrs. Rowney and King to confound other forms with those of Eozoon, accept their determinations in a matter so critical and in a case so unlikely.*

If all specimens of Eozoon were of the acervuline character, the comparison of the chamber-casts with concretionary granules might have some plausibility. But it is to be observed that the laminated arrangement is the typical one; and the study of the larger specimens, cut under the direction of Sir W. E. Logan, shows that these laminated forms must have grown on certain strata-planes before the deposition of the overlying beds, and that the beds are, in part, composed of the broken fragments of similar laminated structures. Further, much of the apparently acervuline Eozoon rock is composed of such broken fragments, the interstices between which should not be confounded with the chambers: while the fact that the serpentine fills such interstices as well as the chambers shows that its arrangement is not concretionary. Again, these chambers are filled in different specimens with serpentine, pyroxene, loganite, calcareous spar, chondrodite, or even with arenaceous limestone. It is also to be observed that the examination of a number of limestones, other than Canadian, by Messrs. King and Rowney, has obliged them to admit that the laminated forms in combination with the canal-system are "essentially Canadian," and that the only instances of structures clearly resembling the Canadian specimens are afforded

* I have since ascertained that Laurentian limestone found at Amity, New York, and containing spinels, does hold fragments of the intermediate skeleton of Eozoon. The limestone may have been originally a mass of fragments of this kind with the aluminous and magnesian material of the spinel in their interstices.

by limestones Laurentian in age, and in some of which (as, for instance, in those of Bavaria and Scandinavia) Carpenter and Gümbel have actually found the structure of Eozoon. The other serpentine-limestones examined (for example, that of Skye) are admitted to fail in essential points of structure; and the only serpentine believed to be of eruptive origin examined by them is confessedly destitute of all semblance of Eozoon. Similar results have been attained by the more careful researches of Prof. Gümbel, whose paper is well deserving of study by all who have any doubts on this subject.

B. REPLY BY DR. HUNT TO CHEMICAL OBJECTIONS—(*Ibid.*).

"In the *Proceedings of the Royal Irish Academy*, for July 12, 1869, Messrs. King and Rowney have given us at length their latest corrected views on various questions connected with Eozoon Canadense. Leaving to my friend, Dr. Dawson, the discussion of the zoological aspects of the question, I cannot forbear making a few criticisms on the chemical and mineralogical views of the authors. The problem which they had before them was to explain the occurrence of certain forms which, to skilled observers, like Carpenter, Dawson, and Rupert Jones, appear to possess all the structural character of the calcareous skeleton of a foraminiferal organism, and moreover to show how it happens that these forms of crystalline carbonate of lime are associated with serpentine in such a way as to lead these observers to conclude that this hydrous silicate of magnesia filled and enveloped the calcareous skeleton, replacing the perishable sarcode. The hypothesis now put forward by Messrs. King and Rowney to explain the appearances in question, is, that all this curiously arranged serpentine, which appears to be a cast of the interior of a complex foraminiferal organism, has been shaped or sculptured out of plates, prisms, and other solids of serpentine, by "the erosion and incomplete waste of the latter, *the definite shapes* being residual portions of the solid that have not completely disappeared." The calcite which limits these definite shapes, or, in other words, what is regarded as the calcareous skeleton of Eozoon, is a 'replacement pseudomorph' of calcite taking the place of the wasted and eroded serpentine. It was not a calcareous fossil, filled and surrounded by the serpentine, but was formed in the midst of the serpentine itself, by a mysterious agency which dissolved away this mineral to form a mould, in which the calcite was cast. This marvellous process can only be paralleled by the operations of that plastic force in virtue of which sea-shells were supposed by some old naturalists to be generated in the midst of rocky strata. Such equivocally formed fossils, whether oysters or Foraminifers, may well be termed *pseudormorphs*, but we are at a loss to see with what propriety the authors of this singular hypothesis invoke the doctrines of mineral pseudormorphism, as taught by Rose, Blum, Bischof, and Dana. In replacement pseudomorphs, as understood by these authors, a mineral species disappears and is replaced by another which retains the external form of the first. Could it be shown that the calcite of the cell-wall of Eozoon was once serpentine, this portion of carbonate of lime would be a replacement pseudomorph after serpentine; but why the portions of this mineral, which on the hypothesis of Messrs. King and Rowney have been thus replaced, should assume the forms of a foraminiferal skeleton, is precisely what our authors fail to show, and, as all must see, is the gist of the whole matter.

"Messrs. King and Rowney, it will be observed, assume the existence of calcite as a replacement pseudomorph after serpentine, but give no evidence of the possibility of such pseudomorphs. Both Rose and Bischof regard serpentine itself as in all cases, of pseudomorphous origin, and as the last result of the changes of a number of mineral species, but give us no example of the pseudomorphous alteration of serpentine itself. It is, according to Bischof, the very insolubility and unalterability of serpentine which cause it to appear as the final result of the change of so many mineral species. Delesse, moreover, in his carefully prepared table of pseudomorphous minerals, in which he has resumed the results of his own and all preceding observers, does not admit the pseudomorphic replacement of serpentine by calcite, nor indeed by any other species.* If, then, such pseudomorphs exist, it appears to be a fact hitherto unobserved, and our authors should at least have given us some evidence of this remarkable case of pseudomorphism by which they seek to support their singular hypothesis.

"I hasten to say, however, that I reject with Scheerer, Delesse and Naumann, a great part of the supposed cases of mineral pseudomorphism, and do not even admit the pseudomorphous origin of serpentine itself, but believe that this, with many other related silicates, has been formed by direct chemical precipitation. This view, which our authors do me the honour to criticise, was set forth by me in 1860 and 1861,† and will be found noticed more in detail in the *Geological Report of Canada*, for 1866, p. 229. I have there and elsewhere maintained that 'steatite, serpentine, pyroxene, hornblende, and in many cases garnet, epidote, and other silicated minerals, are formed by a crystallization and molecular re-arrangement of silicates, generated by chemical processes in waters at the earth's surface.' ‡

"This view, which at once explains the origin of all these bedded rocks, and the fact that their constituent mineral species, like silica and carbonate of lime, replace the perishable matter of organic forms, is designated by Messrs. King and Rowney 'as so completely destitute of the characters of a scientific hypothesis as to be wholly unworthy of consideration, and they speak of my attempt to maintain this hypothesis as 'a total collapse.' How far this statement is from the truth my readers shall judge. My views as to the origin of serpentine and other silicated minerals were set forth by me as above in 1860–1864, before anything was known of the mineralogy of Eozoon, and were forced upon me by my studies of the older crystalline schists of North America. Naumann had already pointed out the necessity of some such hypothesis when he protested against the extravagances of the pseudomorphist

---

* *Annales des Mines*, 5, xvi., 317.
† *Amer. Journ. Science* (2), xxix., 284; xxxii., 286.
‡ *Ibid.*, xxxvii., 266; xxxviii., 183.

school, and maintained that the beds of various silicates found in the crystalline schists are original deposits, and not formed by an epigenic process (*Geognosie*, ii., 65, 154, and *Bull. Soc. Geol. de France*, 2, xviii., 678). This conclusion of Naumann's I have attempted to explain and support by numerous facts and observations, which have led me to the hypothesis in question. Gümbel, who accepts Naumann's view, sustains my hypothesis of the origin of these rocks in a most emphatic manner,* and Credner, in discussing the genesis of the Eozoic rocks, has most ably defended it.† So much for my theoretical views so contemptuously denounced by Messrs. King and Rowney, which are nevertheless unhesitatingly adopted by the two geologists of the time who have made the most special studies of the rocks in question,— Gümbel in Germany, and Credner in North America.

"It would be a thankless task to follow Messrs. King and Rowney through their long paper, which abounds in statements as unsound as those I have just exposed, but I cannot conclude without calling attention to one misconception of theirs as to my view of the origin of limestones. They quote Professor Hull's remark to the effect that the researches of the Canadian geologists and others have shown that the oldest known limestones of the world owe their origin to Eozoon, and remark that the existence of great limestone beds in the Eozoic rocks seems to have influenced Lyell, Ramsay, and others in admitting the received view of Eozoon. Were there no other conceivable source of limestones than Eozoon or similar calcareous skeletons, one might suppose that the presence of such rocks in the Laurentian system could have thus influenced these distinguished geologists, but there are found beneath the Eozoon horizon two great formations of limestone in which this fossil has never been detected. When found, indeed, it owes its conservation in a readily recognisable form to the

* *Proc. Royal Bavarian Acad.* for 1866, translated in *Can. Naturalist*, iii., 81.

† *Die Gliederung der Eozoischen Formations gruppe Nord.-Amerikas,*—a Thesis defended before the *University of Leipzig*, *March* 15, 1869, by Dr. Hermann Credner. Halle, 1869, p. 53.

fact, that it was preserved by the introduction of serpentine at the time of its growth. Above the unbroken Eozoon reefs are limestones made up apparently of the debris of Eozoon thus preserved by serpentine, and there is no doubt that this calcareous rhizopod, growing in water where serpentine was not in process of formation, might, and probably did, build up pure limestone beds like those formed in later times from the ruins of corals and crinoids. Nor is there anything inconsistent in this with the assertion which Messrs. King and Rowney quote from me, viz., that the popular notion that *all limestone formations* owe their origin to organic life is based upon a fallacy. The idea that marine organisms originate the carbonate of lime of their skeletons, in a manner somewhat similar to that in which plants generate the organic matter of theirs, appears to be commonly held among certain geologists. It cannot, however, be too often repeated that animals only appropriate the carbonate of lime which is furnished them by chemical reaction. Were there no animals present to make use of it, the carbonate of lime would accumulate in natural waters till these became saturated, and would then be deposited in an insoluble form; and although thousands of feet of limestone have been formed from the calcareous skeletons of marine animals, it is not less true that great beds of ancient marble, like many modern travertines and tufas, have been deposited without the intervention of life, and even in waters from which living organisms were probably absent. To illustrate this with the parallel case of silicious deposits, there are great beds made up of silicious shields of diatoms. These during their lifetime extracted from the waters the dissolved silica, which, but for their intervention, might have accumulated till it was at length deposited in the form of schist or of crystalline quartz. In either case the function of the coral, the rhizopod, or the diatom is limited to assimilating the carbonate of lime or the silica from its solution, and the organised form thus given to these substances is purely accidental. It is characteristic of our authors, that, rather than admit the limestone beds of the Eozoon rocks to have been formed like beds of coralline limestone, or deposited as chemical precipitates like travertine, they prefer, as they assure us, to regard them as the results of that hitherto unheard-of process, the pseudomorphism of serpentine; as if the deposition of the carbonate of lime in the place of dissolved serpentine were a simpler process than its direct deposition in one or the other of the ways which all the world understands!"

C. Dr. Carpenter on the Foraminiferal Relations of Eozoon.

In the *Annals of Natural History*, for June, 1874, Dr. Carpenter has given a crushing reply to some objections raised in that journal by Mr. Carter. He first shows, contrary to the statement of Mr. Carter, that the fine nummuline tubulation corresponds precisely in its direction with reference to the chambers, with that observed in Nummulites and Orbitoides. In the second place, he shows by clear descriptions and figures, that the relation of the canal system to the fine tubulation is precisely that which he had demonstrated in more recent nummuline and rotaline Foraminifera. In the third place he adduces additional facts to show that in some specimens of Eozoon the calcareous skeleton has been filled with calcite before the introduction of any foreign mineral matter. He concludes the argument in the following words:—

"I have thus shown:—(1) that the 'utter incompatibility' asserted by my opponents to exist between the arrangement of the supposed 'nummuline tubulation' of Eozoon and true Nummuline structure, so far from having any real existence, really furnishes an additional point of conformity; and (2) that three most striking and complete points of conformity exist between the structure of the best-preserved specimens of Eozoon, and that of the Nummulites whose tubulation I described in 1849, and of the Calcarina whose tubulation and canal system I described in 1860.

"That I have not troubled myself to reply to the reiterated arguments in favour of the doctrine [of mineral origin] advanced by Professors King and Rowney on the strength of the occurrence of undoubted results of mineralization in the Canadian Ophite, and of still more marked evidences of the same action in other Ophites, has been simply because these arguments appeared to me, as I thought they must also appear to others, entirely destitute of logical force. Every scientific palæontologist I have ever been acquainted with has taken the *best* preserved specimens, not the *worst*, as the basis of his reconstructions; and if he should meet with distinct evidence of characteristic organic structure in even a very small fragment of a doubtful form, he would consider the organic origin of that form to be thereby substantiated, whatever might be the evidence of purely mineral arrangement which the greater part of his specimen may present,—since he would regard that arrangement as a probable result of *subsequent* mineralization, by which the original organic structure has been more or less obscured. If this is *not* to be our rule of interpretation, a large part of the palæontological work of our time must be thrown aside as worthless. If, for example, Professors King and Rowney were to begin their study of Nummulites by the examination of their most mineralized forms, they would deem themselves justified (according to their canons of interpretation) in denying the existence of the tubulation and canalization which I described (in 1849) in the N. lævigata preserved almost unaltered in the London Clay of Bracklesham Bay.

"My own notions of Eozoic structure have been formed on the examination of the Canadian specimens selected by the experienced discrimination of Sir William Logan, as those in which there was *least* appearance of metamorphism; and having found in these what I regarded as unmistakable evidence of an organic structure conformable to the foraminiferal type, I cannot regard it as any disproof of that conformity, either to show that the true Eozoic structure has been frequently altered by mineral metamorphism, or to adduce the occurrence of Ophites more or less resembling the Eozoon of the Canadian Laurentians at various subsequent geological epochs. The existence of any number or variety of *purely mineral* Ophites would not disprove the organic origin of the Canadian Eozoon —unless it could be shown that some wonderful process of mineralization is competent to construct not only its multiplied alternating lamellæ of calcite and serpentine, the dendritic extensions of the latter into the former, and the 'acicular layer' of decalcified specimens, but (1) the *pre-existing canalization* of the calcareous lamellæ, (2) the *unfilled nummuline tubulation* of the proper wall of the chambers, and (3) the peculiar *calcarine* relation of the canalization and tubulation, here described and figured from specimens in the highest state of preservation, showing the *least* evidence of any mineral change.

"On the other hand, Professors King and Rowney began their studies of Eozoic structure upon the Galway Ophite—a rock which Sir Roderick Murchison described to me at the time as having been so much 'tumbled about,' that he was not at all sure of its geological position, and which exhibits such obvious evidences of mineralization, with such an entire absence of any vestige of organic structure, that I should never for a moment have thought of crediting it with an organic origin, but for the general resemblance of its serpentine-grains to those of the 'acervuline' portion of the Canadian Eozoon. They pronounced with the most positive certainty upon the mineral origin of the Canadian Eozoon, before they had subjected transparent sections of it to any of that careful comparison with similar sections of recent Foraminifera, which had been the basis of Dr. Dawson's original determination, and of my own subsequent confirmation, of its organic structure.

PLATE VIII.

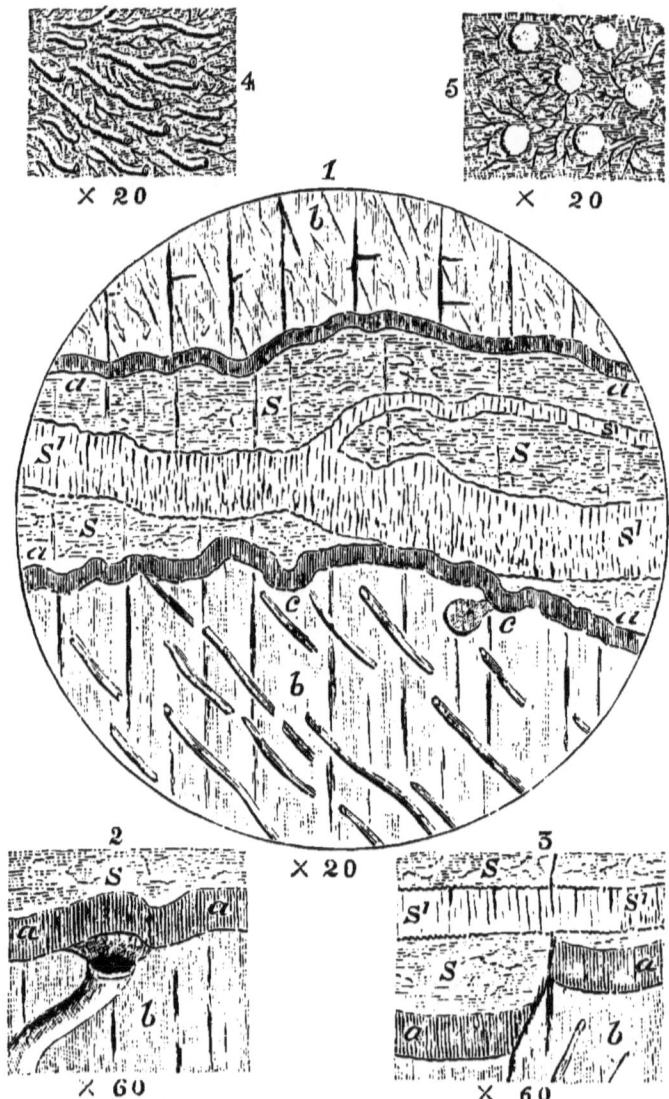

Eozoon and Chrysotile Veins, etc.

FIG. 1.—Portion of two laminæ and intervening serpentine, with chrysotile vein. (*a.*) Proper wall tubulated. (*b.*) Intermediate skeleton, with large canals. (*c.*) Openings of small chamberlets filled with serpentine. (*s.*) Serpentine filling chamber. (s^1.) Vein of chrysotile, showing its difference from the proper wall.

FIG. 2.—Junction of a canal and the proper wall. Lettering as in Fig. 1.

FIG. 3.—Proper wall shifted by a fault, and more recent chrysotile vein not faulted. Lettering as in Fig. 1.

FIG. 4.—Large and small canals filled with dolomite.

FIG. 5.—Abnormally thick portion of intermediate skeleton, with large tubes and small canals filled with dolomite.

CHAPTER VIII.

THE DAWN-ANIMAL AS A TEACHER IN SCIENCE.

THE thoughts suggested to the philosophical naturalist by the contemplation of the dawn of life on our planet are necessarily many and exciting, and the subject has in it the materials for enabling the general reader better to judge of some of the theories of the origin of life agitated in our time. In this respect our dawn-animal has scarcely yet had justice; and we may not be able to render this in these pages. Let us put it into the witness-box, however, and try to elicit its testimony as to the beginnings of life.

Looking down from the elevation of our physiological and mental superiority, it is difficult to realize the exact conditions in which life exists in creatures so simple as the Protozoa. There may perhaps be higher intelligences that find it equally difficult to realize how life and reason can manifest themselves in such poor houses of clay as those we inhabit. But placing ourselves near to these creatures, and entering as it were into sympathy with them, we can understand something of their powers and feelings. In the first place it is plain that they can vigorously, if roughly, exercise those mechanical, chemical, and vegetative powers of life which are characteristic of the animal. They can seize, swallow, digest, and assimilate food; and, employing its albuminous parts in nourishing their tissues, can burn away the rest in processes akin to our respiration, or reject it from their system. Like us, they can subsist only on food which the plant has previously produced; for in this world, from the beginning of time, the plant has been the only organism which could use the solar light and heat as forces to enable it to turn the dead elements of matter into living, growing tissues, and into organic compounds capable of nourishing the animal. Like us, the Protozoa expend the food which they have assimilated in the production of animal force, and in doing so cause it to be oxidized, or burnt away, and resolved again into dead matter. It is true that we have much more complicated apparatus for performing these functions, but it does not follow that this gives us much real superiority, except relatively to the more difficult conditions of our existence. The gourmand who enjoys his dinner may have no more pleasure in the act than the Amœba which swallows a Diatom; and for all that the man knows of the subsequent processes to which the food is subjected, his interior might be a mass of jelly, with extemporised vacuoles, like that of his humble fellow-animal. The workman or the athlete has bones and muscles of vastly complicated structure, but to him the muscular act is as simple and unconscious a process as the sending out of a pseudopod to a Protozoon. The clay is after all the same, and there may be as much credit to the artist in making a simple organism with varied powers, as a more complex frame for doing nicer work. It is a weakness of humanity to plume itself on advantages not of its own making, and to treat its superior gifts as if they were the result of its own endeavours. The truculent traveller who illustrated his boast of superiority over the Indian by comparing his rifle with the bow and arrows of the savage, was well answered by the question, "Can you make a rifle?" and when he had to answer, "No," by the rejoinder, "Then I am at least better than you, for I can make my bow and arrows." The Amœba or the Eozoon is probably no more than we its own creator; but if it could produce itself out of vegetable matter or out of inorganic substances, it might claim in so far a higher place in the scale of being than we; and as it is, it can assert equal powers of digestion, assimilation, and motion, with much less of bodily mechanism.

In order that we may feel, a complicated apparatus of nerves and brain-cells has to be constructed and set to work; but the Protozoon, without any distinct brain, is all brain, and its sensation is simply direct. Thus vision in these creatures is probably performed in a rough way by any part of their transparent bodies, and taste and smell are no doubt in the same case. Whether they have any perception of sound as distinct from the mere vibrations ascertained by touch, we do not know. Here also we are not far removed above the Protozoa, especially those of us to whom touch, seeing, and hearing are mere feelings, without thought or knowledge of the apparatus employed. We might so far as well be Amœbas. As we rise higher we meet with more differences. Yet it is evident that our gelatinous fellow-being can feel pain, dread danger, desire possessions, enjoy pleasure, and in a simple unconscious way entertain many of the appetites and passions that affect ourselves. The wonder is that with so little of organization it can do so much. Yet, perhaps, life can manifest itself in a broader and more intense way where there is little organization; and a highly strung and complex organism is not so much a necessary condition of a higher life as a mere means of better adapting it to its present surroundings. Those philosophies which identify the thinking mind with the material organism, must seem outrageous blunders to an Amœba on the one hand, or to an angel on the other, could either be enabled to understand them; which, however, is not very probable, as they are too intimately bound up with the mere prejudices incident to the present condition of our humanity. In any case the Protozoa teach us how much of animal function may be fulfilled by a very simple organism, and warn us against the fallacy that creatures of this simple structure are necessarily nearer to inorganic matter, and more easily developed from it than beings of more complex mould.

A similar lesson is taught by the complexity of their skeletons. We speak in a crude unscientific way of these animals accumulating calcareous matter, and building up reefs of limestone. We must, however, bear in mind that they are as dependent on their food for the materials of their skeletons as we are, and that their crusts grow in the interior of the sarcode just as our bones do within our bodies. The provision even for nourishing the interior of the skeleton by tubuli and canals is in principle similar to that involved in the Haversian canals, cells, and canalicules of bone. The Amœba of course knows neither more nor less of this than the average Englishman. It is altogether a matter of unconscious growth. The process in the Protozoa strikes some minds, however, as the more wonderful of the two. It is, says an eminent modern physiologist, a matter of "profound significance" that this "particle of jelly [the sarcode of a Foraminifer] is capable of guiding physical forces in such a manner as to give rise to these exquisite and almost mathematically arranged structures." Respecting the structures themselves there is no exaggeration in this. No arch or dome framed by human skill is more perfect in beauty or in the realization of mechanical ideas than the tests of some Foraminifera, and none is so complete and wonderful in its internal structure. The particle of jelly, however, is a figure of speech. The body of the humblest Foraminifer is much more than this. It is an organism with divers parts, as we have already seen in a previous chapter, and it is endowed with the mysterious forces of life which in it guide the physical forces, just as they do in building up phosphate of lime in our bones, or indeed just as the will of the architect does in building a palace. The profound significance which this has, reaches beyond the domain of the physical and vital, even to the spiritual. It clings to all our conceptions of living things: quite as much, for example, to the evolution of an animal with all its parts from a one-celled germ, or to the connection of brain-cells with the manifestations of intelligence. Viewed in this way, we may share with the author of the sentence I have quoted his feeling of veneration in the presence of this great wonder of animal life, "burning, and not consumed," nay, building up, and that in many and beautiful forms. We may realize it most of all in the presence of the organism which was perhaps the first to manifest on our planet these marvellous powers. We must, however, here also, beware of that credulity which makes too many thinkers limit their conceptions altogether to physical force in matters of this kind. The merely materialistic physiologist is really in no better position than the savage who quails before the thunderstorm, or rejoices in the solar warmth, and seeing no force or power beyond, fancies himself in the immediate presence of his God. In Eozoon we must discern not only a mass of jelly, but a being endowed with that higher vital force which surpasses vegetable life and also physical and chemical forces; and in this animal energy we must see an emanation from a Will higher than our own, ruling vitality itself; and this not merely to the end of constructing the skeleton of a Protozoon, but of elaborating all the wonderful developments of life that were to follow in succeeding ages, and with reference to which the production and growth of this creature were initial steps. It is this mystery of design which really constitutes the "profound significance" of the foraminiferal skeleton.

Another phenomenon of animality forced upon our notice by the Protozoa is that of the conditions of life in animals not individual, as we are, but aggregative and cumulative in indefinite masses. What, for instance, the relations to each other of the Polyps, growing together in a coral mass, of the separate parts of a Sponge, or the separate cells of a Foraminifer, or of the sarcode mass of an indefinitely spread out Stromatopora or Bathybius. In the case of the Polyps, we may believe that there is special sensation in the tentacles and oral opening of each individual, and that each may experience hunger when in want, or satisfaction when it is filled with food, and that injuries to one part of the mass may indirectly affect other parts, but that the nutrition of the whole mass may be as much unfelt by the individual Polyps as the processes going on in our own bones are by us. So in the case of a large Sponge or Foraminifer, there may be some special sensation in individual cells, pseudopods, or segments, and the general sensation may be very limited, while unconscious living powers pervade the whole. In this matter of aggregation of animals we have thus various grades. The Foraminifers and Sponges present us with the simplest of all, and that which most resembles the aggregation of buds in the plant. The Polyps and complex Bryozoons present a higher and more specialised type; and though the bilateral symmetry which obtains in the higher animals is of a different nature, it still at least reminds us of that multiplication of similar parts which we see in the lower grades of being. It is worthy of notice here that the lower animals which show aggregative tendencies present but imperfect indications, or none at all, of bilateral symmetry. Their bodies, like those of plants, are for the most part built up around a central axis, or they show tendencies to spiral modes of growth.

It is this composite sort of life which is connected with the main geological function of the Foraminifer. While active sensation, appetite, and enjoyment pervade the pseudopods and external sarcode of the mass, the hard skeleton common to the whole is growing within; and in this way the calcareous matter is gradually removed from the sea water, and built up in solid reefs, or in piles of loose foraminiferal shells. Thus it is the aggregative or common life, alike in Foraminifers as in Corals, that tends most powerfully to the accumulation of calcareous matter; and those creatures whose life is of this complex character are best suited to be world-builders, since the result of their growth is not merely a cemetery of their osseous remains, but a huge communistic edifice, to which multitudes of lives have contributed, and in which successive generations take up their abode on the remains of their ancestors. This process, so potent in the progress of the earth's geological history, began, as far as we know, with Eozoon.

Whether, then, in questioning our proto-foraminifer, we have reference to the vital functions of its gelatinous sarcode, to the complexity and beauty of its calcareous test, or to its capacity for effecting great material results through the union of individuals, we perceive that we have to do, not with a low condition of those powers which we designate life, but with the manifestation of those powers through the means of a simple organism; and this in a degree of perfection which we, from our point of view, would have in the first instance supposed impossible.

If we imagine a world altogether destitute of life, we still might have geological formations in progress. Not only would volcanoes belch forth their liquid lavas and their stones and ashes, but the waves and currents of the ocean and the rains and streams on the land, with the ceaseless decomposing action of the carbonic acid of the atmosphere, would be piling up mud, sand, and pebbles in the sea. There might even be some formation of limestone taking place where springs charged with bicarbonate of lime were oozing out on the land or the bottom of the waters. But in such a world all the carbon would be in the state of carbonic acid, and all the limestone would either be diffused in small quantities through various rocks or in limited local beds, or in solution, perhaps as chloride of calcium, in the sea. Dr. Hunt has given chemical grounds for supposing that the most ancient seas were largely supplied with this very soluble salt, instead of the chloride of sodium, or common salt, which now prevails in the sea-water.

Where in such a world would life be introduced? on the land or in the waters? All scientific probability would say in the latter. The ocean is now vastly more populous than the land. The waters alone afford the conditions necessary at once for the most minute and the grandest organisms, at once for the simplest and for others of the most complex character. Especially do they afford the best conditions for those animals which subsist in complex communities, and which aggregate large quantities of mineral matter in their skeletons. So true is this that up to the present time all the species of Protozoa and of the animals most nearly allied to them are aquatic. Even in the waters, however, plant life, though possibly in very simple forms, must precede the animal.

Let humble plants, then, be introduced in the waters, and they would at once begin to use the solar light for the purpose of decomposing carbonic acid, and forming carbon compounds which had not before existed, and which independently of vegetable life would never have existed. At the same time lime and other mineral substances present in the sea-water would be fixed in the tissues of these plants, either in a minute state of division, as little grains or Coccoliths, or in more solid masses like those of the Corallines and Nullipores. In this way a beginning of limestone formation might be made, and quantities of carbonaceous and bituminous matter, resulting from the decay of marine plants might accumulate in the sea-bottom. Now arises the opportunity for animal life. The plants have collected stores of organic matter, and their minute germs, along with microscopic species, are floating everywhere in the sea. Nay, there may be abundant examples of those Amœba-like germs of aquatic plants, simulating for a time the life of the animal, and then returning into the circle of vegetable life. In these some might see precursors of the Protozoa, though they are probably rather prophetic analogues than blood relations. The plant has fulfilled its function as far as the waters are concerned, and now arises the opportunity for the animal. In what form shall it appear? Many of its higher forms, those which depend upon animal food or on the more complex plants for subsistence, would obviously be unsuitable. Further, the sea-water is still too much saturated with saline matter to be fit for the higher animals of the waters. Still further, there may be a residue of internal heat forbidding coolness, and that solution of free oxygen which is an essential condition of existence to most of the modern animals. Something must be found suitable for this saline, imperfectly oxygenated, tepid sea. Something too is wanted that can aid in introducing conditions more favourable to higher life in the future. Our experience of the modern world shows us that all these conditions can be better fulfilled by the Protozoa than by any other creatures. They can live now equally in those great depths of ocean where the conditions are most unfavourable to other forms of life, and in tepid unhealthy pools overstocked with vegetable matter in a state of putridity. They form a most suitable basis for higher forms of life. They have remarkable powers of removing mineral matters from the waters and of fixing them in solid forms. So in the fitness of things Eozoon is just what we need, and after it has spread itself over the mud and rock of the primeval seas, and built up extensive reefs therein, other animals may be introduced capable of feeding on it, or of sheltering themselves in its stony masses, and thus we have the appropriate dawn of animal life.

But what are we to say of the cause of this new series of facts, so wonderfully superimposed upon the merely vegetable and mineral? Must it remain to us as an act of creation, or was it derived from some preexisting matter in which it had been potentially present? Science fails to inform us, but conjectural "phylogeny" steps in and takes its place. Haeckel, the prophet of this new philosophy, waves his magic wand, and simple masses of sarcode spring from inorganic matter, and form diffused sheets of sea-slime, from which are in time separated distinct Amœboid and Foraminiferal forms. Experience, however, gives us no facts whereon to build this supposition, and it remains neither more nor less scientific or certain than that old fancy of the Egyptians, which derived animals from the fertile mud of the Nile.

If we fail to learn anything of the origin of Eozoon,

and if its life-processes are just as inscrutable as those of higher creatures, we can at least inquire as to its history in geological time. In this respect we find in the first place that the Protozoa have not had a monopoly in their profession of accumulators of calcareous rock. Originated by Eozoon in the old Laurentian time, this process has been proceeding throughout the geological ages; and while Protozoa, equally simple with the great prototype of the race, have been and are continuing its function, and producing new limestones in every geological period, and so adding to the volume of the successive formations, new workers of higher grades have been introduced, capable of enjoying higher forms of animal activity, and equally of labouring at the great task of continent-building; of existing, too, in seas less rich in mineral substances than those of the Eozoic time, and for that very reason better suited to higher and more skilled artists. It is to be observed in connection with this, that as the work of the Foraminifers has thus been assumed by others, their size and importance have diminished, and the grander forms of more recent times have some of them been fain to build up their hard parts of cemented sand instead of limestone.

But we further find that, while the first though not the only organic gatherers of limestone from the ocean waters, they have had to do, not merely with the formation of calcareous sediments, but also with that of silicious deposits. The greenish silicate called glauconite, or greensand, is found to be associated with much of the foraminiferal slime now accumulating in the ocean, and also with the older deposits of this kind now consolidated in chalks and similar rocks. This name glauconite is, as Dr. Hunt has shown, employed to designate not only the hydrous silicate of iron and potash, which perhaps has the best right to it, but also compounds which contain in addition large percentages of alumina, or magnesia, or both; and one glauconite from the Tertiary limestones near Paris, is said to be a true serpentine, or hydrous silicate of magnesia.* Now the association of such substances with Foraminifera is not purely accidental. Just as a fragment of decaying wood, imbedded in sediment, has the power of decomposing soluble silicates carried to it by water, and parting with its carbon in the form of carbonic acid, in exchange for the silica, and thus replacing, particle by particle, the carbon of the wood with silicon, so that at length it becomes petrified into a flinty mass, so the sarcode of a Foraminifer, which is a more dense kind of animal matter than is usually supposed, can in like manner abstract silica from the surrounding water or water-soaked sediment. From some peculiarity in the conditions of the case, however, our Protozoon usually becomes petrified with a hydrous silicate instead of with pure silica. The favourable conditions presented by the deep sea for the combination of silica with bases, may perhaps account in part

* Berthier, quoted by Hunt.

for this. But whatever the cause, it is usual to find fossil Foraminifera with their sarcode replaced by such material. We also find beds of glauconite retaining the forms of Foraminifera, while the calcareous tests of these have been removed, apparently by acid waters.

One consideration which, though conjectural, deserves notice, is connected with the food of these humble animals. They are known to feed to a large extent on minute plants, the Diatoms, and other organisms having silica in their skeletons or cell-walls, and consequently soluble silicates in their juices. The silicious matter contained in these organisms is not wanted by the Foraminifera for their own skeletons, and will therefore be voided by them as an excrementitious matter. In this way, where Foraminifera greatly abound, there may be a large production of soluble silica and silicates, in a condition ready to enter into new and insoluble compounds, and to fill the cavities and pores of dead shells. Thus glauconite and even serpentine may, in a certain sense, be a sort of foraminiferal coprolitic matter or excrement. Of course it is not necessary to suppose that this is the only source of such materials. They may be formed in other ways; but I suggest this as at least a possible link of connection.

Whether or not the conjecture last mentioned has any validity, there is another and most curious bond of connection between oceanic Protozoa and silicious deposits. Professor Wyville Thompson reports from the *Challenger* soundings, that in certain areas of the South Pacific the ordinary foraminiferal ooze is replaced by a peculiar red clay, which he attributes to the action of water laden with carbonic acid, in removing all the lime, and leaving this red mud as a sort of ash, composed of silica, alumina, and iron oxide. Now this is in all probability a product of the decomposition and oxidation of the glauconitic matter contained in the ooze. Thus we learn that when areas on which calcareous deposits have been accumulated by Protozoa, are invaded by cold arctic or antarctic waters charged with carbonic acid, the carbonate of lime may be removed, and the glauconite left, or even the latter may be decomposed, leaving silicious, aluminous, and other deposits, which may be quite destitute of any organic structures, or retain only such remnants of them as have been accidentally or by their more resisting character protected from destruction.* In this way it may be possible that many silicious rocks of the Laurentian and Primordial ages, which now show no trace of organization, may be

---

* The "red chalk" of Antrim, and that of Speeton, contain arenaceous Foraminifera and silicious casts of their shells, apparently different from typical glauconite, and the extremely fine ferruginous and argillaceous sediment of these chalks may well be decomposed glauconitic matter like that of the South Pacific. I have found these beds, the hard limestones of the French Neocomian, and the altered greensands of the Alps, very instructive for comparison with the Laurentian limestones; and they well deserve study by all interested in such subjects.

indirectly products of the action of life. When the recent deposits discovered by the *Challenger* dredgings shall have been more fully examined, we may perhaps have the means of distinguishing such rocks, and thus of still further enlarging our conceptions of the part played by Protozoa in the drama of the earth's history. In any case it seems plain that beds of greensand and similar hydrous silicates may be the residue of thick deposits of foraminiferal limestone or chalky matter, and that these silicates may in their turn be oxidised and decomposed, leaving beds of apparently inorganic clay. Such beds may finally be consolidated and rendered crystalline by metamorphism, and thus a great variety of silicated rocks may result, retaining little or no indication of any connection with the agency of life. We can scarcely yet conjecture the amount of light which these new facts may eventually throw on the serpentine and other rocks of the Eozoic age. In the meantime they open up a noble field to chemists and microscopists.

When the marvellous results of recent deep-sea dredgings were first made known, and it was found that chalky foraminiferal earth is yet accumulating in the Atlantic, with sponges and sea urchins resembling in many respects those whose remains exist in the chalk, the fact was expressed by the statement that we still live in the chalk period. Thus stated the conclusion is scarcely correct. We do not live in the chalk period, but the conditions of the chalk period still exist in the deep sea. We may say more than this. To some extent the conditions of the Laurentian period still exist in the sea, except in so far as they have been removed by the action of the Foraminifera and other limestone builders. To those who can realize the enormous lapse of time involved in the geological history of the earth, this conveys an impression almost of eternity in the existence of this oldest of all the families of the animal kingdom.

We are still more deeply impressed with this when we bring into view the great physical changes which have occurred since the dawn of life. When we consider that the skeletons of Eozoon contribute to form the oldest hills of our continents; that they have been sealed up in solid marble, and that they are associated with hard crystalline rocks contorted in the most fantastic manner; that these rocks have almost from the beginning of geological time been undergoing waste to supply the material of new formations; that they have witnessed innumerable subsidences and elevations of the continents; and that the greatest mountain chains of the earth have been built up from the sea since Eozoon began to exist,—we acquire a most profound impression of the persistence of the lower forms of animal life, and know that mountains may be removed and continents swept away and replaced, before the least of the humble gelatinous Protozoa can finally perish. Life may be a fleeting thing in the individual, but as handed down through successive generations of beings, and as a constant animating power in successive organisms, it appears, like its Creator, eternal.

This leads to another and very serious question. How long did lineal descendants of Eozoon exist, and do they still exist? We may for the present consider this question apart from ideas of derivation and elevation into higher planes of existence. Eozoon as a species and even as a genus may cease to exist with the Eozoic age, and we have no evidence whatever that Archæocyathus, Stromatopora, or Receptaculites are its modified descendants. As far as their structures inform us, they may as much claim to be original creations as Eozoon itself. Still descendants of Eozoon may have continued to exist, though we have not yet met with them. I should not be surprised to hear of a veritable specimen being some day dredged alive in the Atlantic or the Pacific. It is also to be observed that in animals so simple as Eozoon many varieties may appear, widely different from the original. In these the general form and habit of life are the most likely things to change, the minute structures much less so. We need not, therefore, be surprised to find its descendants diminishing in size or altering in general form, while the characters of the fine tubulation and of the canal system would remain. We need not wonder if any sessile Foraminifer of the Nummuline group should prove to be a descendant of Eozoon. It would be less likely that a Sponge or a Foraminifer of the Rotaline type should originate from it. If one could only secure a succession of deep-sea limestones with Foraminifers, extending all the way from the Laurentian to the present time, I can imagine nothing more interesting than to compare the whole series, with the view of ascertaining the limits of descent with variation, and the points where new forms are introduced. We have not yet such a series, but it may be obtained; and as Foraminifera are eminently cosmopolitan, occurring over vastly wide areas of sea-bottom, and are very variable, they would afford a better test of theories of derivation than any that can be obtained from the more locally distributed and less variable animals of higher grade. I was much struck with this recently, in examining a series of Foraminifera from the Cretaceous of Manitoba, and comparing them with the varietal forms of the same species in the interior of Nebraska, 500 miles to the south, and with those of the English chalk and of the modern seas. In all these different times and places we had the same species. In all they existed under so many varietal forms passing into each other, that in former times every species had been multiplied into several. Yet in all, the identical varietal forms were repeated with the most minute markings alike. Here were at once constancy the most remarkable and variations the most extensive. If we dwell on the one to the exclusion of the other, we reach only one-sided conclusions, imperfect and unsatisfactory. By taking both in connection we can alone realize the full significance of the facts. We cannot yet obtain such series for all geological time; but it may even now be worth while to inquire, What do we know as to any modification in the case of the primeval Foraminifers, whether with reference to the derivation from them of other Protozoa or of higher forms of life?

There is no link whatever in geological fact to connect Eozoon with any of the Mollusks, Radiates, or Crustaceans of the succeeding Primordial. What may be discovered in the future we cannot conjecture; but at present these stand before us as distinct creations. It would of course be more probable that Eozoon should be the ancestor of some of the Foraminifera of the Primordial age, but strangely enough it is very dissimilar from all these except Stromatopora; and here, as already stated, the evidence of minute structure fails to a great extent, and Eozoon Bavaricum of the Huronian age scarcely helps to bridge over the gap which yawns in our imperfect geological record. Of actual facts, therefore, we have none; and those evolutionists who have regarded the dawn-animal as an evidence in their favour, have been obliged to have recourse to supposition and assumption.

Taking the ground of the derivationist, it is convenient to assume (1) that Eozoon was either the first or nearly the first of animals, and that, being a Protozoan of simple structure, it constitutes an appropriate beginning of life; (2) that it originated from some unexplained change in the protoplasmic or albuminous matter of some humble plant, or directly from inorganic matter, or at least was descended from some creature only a little more simple which had being in this way; (3) that it had in itself unlimited capacities for variation and also for extension in time; (4) that it tended to multiply rapidly, and at last so to occupy the ocean that a struggle for existence arose; (5) that though at first, from the very nature of its origin, adapted to the conditions of the world, yet as these conditions became altered by physical changes, it was induced to accommodate itself to them, and so to pass into new species and genera, until at last it appeared in entirely new types in the Primordial fauna.

These assumptions are, with the exception of the first two, merely the application to Eozoon of what have been called the Darwinian laws of multiplication, of limited population, of variation, of change of physical conditions, and of equilibrium of nature. If otherwise proved, and shown to be applicable to creatures like Eozoon, of course we must apply them to it; but in so far as that creature itself is concerned they are incapable of proof, and some of them contrary to such evidence as we have. We have, for example, no connecting link between Eozoon and any form of vegetable life. Its structures are such as to enable us at once to assign it to the animal kingdom, and if we seek for connecting links between the lower animals and plants we have to look for them in the modern waters. We have no reason to conclude that Eozoon could multiply so rapidly as to fill all the stations suitable for it, and to commence a struggle for existence. On the contrary, after the lapse of untold ages the conditions for the life of Foraminifers still exist over two-thirds of the surface of the earth. In regard to variation, we have, it is true, evidence of the wide range of varieties of species in Protozoa, within the limits of the group, but none whatever of any tendency to pass into other groups. Nor can it be proved that the conditions of the ocean were so different in Cambrian or Silurian times as to preclude the continued and comfortable existence of Eozoon. New creatures came in which superseded it, and new conditions more favourable in proportion to these new creatures, but neither the new creatures nor the new conditions were necessarily or probably connected with Eozoon, any farther than that it may have served newer tribes of animals for food, and may have rid the sea of some of its superfluous lime in their interest. In short, the hypothesis of evolution will explain the derivation of other animals from Eozoon if we adopt its assumptions, just as it will in that case explain anything else, but the assumptions are improbable, and contrary to such facts as we know.

Eozoon itself, however, bears some negative though damaging testimony against evolution, and its argument may be thus stated in what we may imagine to be its own expressions :—" I, Eozoon Canadense, being a creature of low organization and intelligence, and of practical turn, am no theorist, but have a lively appreciation of such facts as I am able to perceive. I found myself growing upon the sea-bottom, and know not whence I came. I grew and flourished for ages, and found no let or hindrance to my expansion, and abundance of food was always floated to me without my having to go in search of it. At length a change came. Certain creatures with hard snouts and jaws began to prey on me. Whence they came I know not; I cannot think that they came from the germs which I had dispersed so abundantly throughout the ocean. Unfortunately, just at the same time lime became a little less abundant in the waters, perhaps because of the great demands I myself had made, and thus it was not so easy as before to produce a thick supplemental skeleton for defence. So I had to give way. I have done my best to avoid extinction; but it is clear that I must at length be overcome, and must either disappear or subside into a humbler condition, and that other creatures better provided for the new conditions of the world must take my place." In such terms we may suppose that this patriarch of the seas might tell his history, and mourn his destiny, though he might also congratulate himself on having in an honest way done his duty and fulfilled his function in the world, leaving it to other and perhaps wiser creatures to dispute as to his origin and fate, while much less perfectly fulfilling the ends of their own existence.

Thus our dawn-animal has positively no story to tell as to his own introduction or his transmutation into other forms of existence. He leaves the mystery of creation where it was; but in connection with the subsequent history of life we can learn from him a little as to the laws which have governed the succession of animals in geological time. First, we may learn that the plan of creation has been progressive, that there has been an advance from the few, low, and generalized types of the primæval ocean to the more numerous, higher, and more specialized types of more recent times. Secondly, we learn that the lower types, when first introduced, and before they were subordinated to higher forms of life, existed in some of their grandest modifications as to form and complexity, and that in succeeding ages, when higher types were replacing them, they were subjected to decay and degeneracy. Thirdly, we learn that while the species has a limited term of existence in geological time, any grand type of animal existence, like that of the Foraminifera or Sponges, for example, once introduced, continues and finds throughout all the vicissitudes of the earth some appropriate residence. Fourthly, as to the mode of introduction of new types, or whether such creatures as Eozoon had any direct connection with the subsequent introduction of mollusks, worms, or crustaceans, it is altogether silent, nor can it predict anything as to the order or manner of their introduction.

Had we been permitted to visit the Laurentian seas, and to study Eozoon and its contemporary Protozoa when alive, it is plain that we could not have foreseen or predicted from the consideration of such organisms the future development of life. No amount of study of the prototypal Foraminifer could have led us distinctly to the conception of even a Sponge or a Polyp, much less of any of the higher animals. Why is this?

The answer is that the improvement into such higher types does not take place by any change of the elementary sarcode, either in those chemical, mechanical, or vital properties which we can study, but in the adding to it of new structures. In the Sponge, which is perhaps the nearest type of all, we have the movable pulsating cilium and true animal cellular tissue, and along with this the spicular or fibrous skeleton, these structures leading to an entire change in the mode of life and subsistence. In the higher types of animals it is the same. Even in the highest we have white blood-corpuscles and germinal matter, which, in so far as we know, carry on no higher forms of life than those of an Amœba; but they are now made subordinate to other kinds of tissue, of great variety and complexity, which never have been observed to arise out of the growth of any Protozoon. There would be only a very few conceivable inferences which the highest finite intelligence could deduce as to the development of future and higher animals. He might infer that the foraminiferal sarcode, once introduced, might be the substratum or foundation of other but unknown tissues in the higher animals, and that the Protozoan type might continue to subsist side by side with higher forms of living things as they were successively introduced. He might also infer that the elevation of the animal kingdom would take place with reference to those new properties of sensation and voluntary motion in which the humblest animals diverge from the life of the plant.

It is important that these points should be clearly before our minds, because there has been current of late among naturalists a loose way of writing with reference to them, which seems to have imposed on many who are not naturalists. It has been said, for example, that such an organism as Eozoon may include potentially all the structures and functions of the higher animals, and that it is possible that we might be able to infer or calculate all these with as much certainty as we can calculate an eclipse or any other physical phenomenon. Now, there is not only no foundation in fact for these assertions, but it is from our present standpoint not conceivable that they can ever be realized. The laws of inorganic matter give no data whence any *à priori* deductions or calculations could be made as to the structure and vital forces of the plant. The plant gives no data from which we can calculate the functions of the animal. The Protozoon gives no data from which we can calculate the specialties of the Mollusc, the Articulate, or the Vertebrate. Nor unhappily do the present conditions of life of themselves give us any sure grounds for predicting the new creations that may be in store for our old planet. Those who think to build a philosophy and even a religion on such data are mere dreamers, and have no scientific basis for their dogmas. They are more blind guides than our primæval Protozoon himsel would be, in matters whose real solution lies in the harmony of our own higher and immaterial nature with the Being who is the author of all life—the

Father "from whom every family in heaven and earth is named."

While this work was going through the press, Lyell, the greatest geological thinker of our time, passed away. In the preceding pages I have refrained from quoting the many able geologists and biologists who have publicly accepted the evidence of the animal nature of Eozoon as sufficient, preferring to rest my case on its own merits rather than on authority; but it is due to the great man whose loss we now mourn, to say that, before the discovery of Eozoon, he had expressed on general grounds his anticipation that fossils would be found in the rocks older than the so-called Primordial Series, and that he at once admitted the organic nature of Eozoon, and introduced it, as a fossil, into the edition of his Elements of Geology published in the same year in which it was described.

APPENDIX.

CHARACTERS OF LAURENTIAN AND HURONIAN PROTOZOA.

It may be useful to students to state the technical characters of Eozoon, in addition to the more popular and general descriptions in the preceding pages.

Genus EOZOON.

Foraminiferal skeletons, with irregular and often confluent cells, arranged in concentric and horizontal laminæ, or sometimes piled in an acervuline manner. Septal orifices irregularly disposed. Proper wall finely tubulated. Intermediate skeleton with branching canals.

Eozoon Canadense, *Dawson*.

In rounded masses or thick encrusting sheets, frequently of large dimensions. Typical structure stromatoporoid, or with concentric calcareous walls, frequently uniting with each other, and separating flat chambers, more or less mammillated, and spreading into horizontal lobes and small chamberlets; chambers often confluent and crossed by irregular calcareous pillars connecting the opposite walls. Upper part often composed of acervuline chambers of rounded forms. Proper wall tubulated very finely. Intermediate skeleton largely developed, especially at the lower part, and traversed by large canals, often with smaller canals in their interstices. Lower laminæ and chambers often three millimetres in thickness. Upper laminæ and chambers one millimetre or less. Age Laurentian and perhaps Huronian.

Var. MINOR.—Supplemental skeleton wanting, except near the base, and with very fine canals. Laminæ of sarcode much mammillated, thin, and separated by very thin walls. Probably a depauperated variety.

Var. ACERVULINA.—In oval or rounded masses, wholly acervuline. Cells rounded; intermediate skeleton absent or much reduced; cell-walls tubulated. This may be a distinct species, but it closely resembles the acervuline parts of the ordinary form.

EOZOON BAVARICUM, *Gümbel.*

Composed of small acervuline chambers, separated by contorted walls, and associated with broad plate-like chambers below. Large canals in the thicker parts of the intermediate skeleton. Differs from *E. Canadense* in its smaller and more contorted chambers. Age probably Huronian.

Genus ARCHÆOSPHERINA.

A provisional genus, to include rounded solitary chambers, or globigerine assemblages of such chambers, with the cell-wall surrounding them tubulated as in Eozoon. They may be distinct organisms, or gemmæ or detached fragments of Eozoon. Some of them much resemble the bodies figured by Dr. Carpenter, as gemmæ or ova and primitive chambers of Orbitolites. They are very abundant on some of the strata surfaces of the limestone at Côte St. Pierre. Age Lower Laurentian.

SYSTEMATIC POSITION OF EOZOON.

The unsettled condition of the classification of the Protozoa, and our absolute ignorance of the animal matter of Eozoon, render it difficult to make any statement on this subject more definite than the somewhat vague intimations given in the text. My own views at present, based on the study of recent and fossil forms, and of the writings of Carpenter, Max Schultze, Carter, Wallich, Haeckel, and Clarepede, may be stated, though with some diffidence, as follows:—

I. The class *Rhizopoda* includes all the sarcodous animals whose only external organs are pseudopodia, and is the lowest class in the animal kingdom. Immediately above it are the classes of the Sponges and of the flagellate and ciliate Infusoria, which rise from it like two diverging branches.

II. The group of Rhizopods, as thus defined, includes three leading *orders*, which, in descending grade, are as follows:—

(a) *Lobosa*, or Amœboid Rhizopods, including those with distinct nucleus and pulsating vesicle, and thick lobulate pseudopodia—naked, or in membranous coverings.

(b) *Radiolaria*, or Polycistius and their allies, including those with thread-like pseudopodia, with or without a nucleus, and with the skeleton, when present, silicious.

(c) *Reticularia*, or Foraminifera and their allies, including those with thread-like and reticulating pseudopodia, with granular matter instead of a nucleus, and with calcareous, membranous, or arenaceous skeletons.

The place of *Eozoon* will be in the lowest order, *Reticularia*.

III. The order *Reticularia* may be farther divided into two *sub-orders*, as follows:—

(a) *Perforata*—having calcareous skeletons penetrated with pores.

(b) *Imperforata*—having calcareous, membranous, or arenaceous skeletons, without pores.

The place of Eozoon will be in the higher sub-order, *Perforata*.

IV. The sub-order *Perforata* includes three *families*—the *Nummulinidæ*, *Globigerinidæ*, and *Lagenidæ*. Of these Carpenter regards the Nummulinidæ as the highest in rank.

The place of Eozoon will be in the family *Nummulinidæ*, or between this and the next family. This oldest known Protozoon would thus belong to the highest family in the highest sub-order of the lowest class of animals.

THE LATE SIR WILLIAM E. LOGAN.

WHEN writing the dedication of this work, I little thought that the eminent geologist and valued friend to whom it gave me so much pleasure to tender this tribute of respect, would have passed away before its publication. But so it is, and we have now to mourn, not only Lyell, who so frankly accepted the evidence in favour of Eozoon, but Logan, who so boldly from the first maintained its true nature as a fossil. This boldness on his part is the more remarkable and impressive, from the extreme caution by which he was characterized, and which induced him to take the most scrupulous pains to verify every new fact before committing himself to it. Though Sir William's early work in the Welsh coal-fields, his organization and management of the Survey of Canada, and his reducing to order for the first time all the widely extended Palæozoic formations of that great country, must always constitute leading elements in his reputation, I think that in nothing does he deserve greater credit than in the skill and genius with which he attacked the difficult problem of the Laurentian rocks, unravelled their intricacies, and ascertained their true nature as sediments, and the leading facts of their arrangement and distribution. The discovery of Eozoon was one of the results of this great work; and it was the firm conviction to which Sir William had attained of the sedimentary character of the rocks, which rendered his mind open to the evidence of these contained fossils, and induced him even to expect the discovery of them.

This would not be the proper place to dwell on the general character and work of Sir William Logan, but I cannot close without referring to his untiring industry, his enthusiasm in the investigation of nature, his cheerful and single-hearted disposition, his earnest public spirit and patriotism—qualities which won for him the regard even of those who could little appreciate the details of his work, and which did much to enable him to attain to the success which he achieved.

INDEX.

Acervuline explained, 66.
Acervuline Variety of Eozoon, 135.
Aggregative Growth of Animals, 213.
Aker Limestone, 197.
Amity Limestone, 197.
Amœba described, 59.
Annelid Burrows, 133, 139.
Archæospherinæ, 137, 148.
Archæocyathus, 151.
Arisaig, Supposed Eozoon of, 140.

Bathybius, 65.
Bavaria, Eozoon of, 148.
Beginning of Life, 215.
Billings, Mr.,—referred to, 41; on Archæocyathus, 151; on Receptaculites, 163.

Calumet, Eozoon of, 38.
Calcarina, 74.
Calcite filling Tubes of Eozoon, 98.
Canal System of Eozoon, 40, 66, 107, 176, 181.
Carpenter—referred to, 41; on Eozoon, 82; Reply to Carter, 204.
Caunopora, 158.
Chrysotile Veins, 107, 180.
Chemistry of Eozoon, 199.
Coccoliths, 70.

Cœnostroma, 158.
Contemporaries of Eozoon, 127.
Côte St. Pierre, 20.

Derivation applied to Eozoon, 225.
Discovery of Eozoon, 35.

Eozoic Time, 7.
Eozoon,—Discovery of, 35 ; Structure of, 65; Growth of, 70 ; Fragments of, 74 ; Description of, 65, 77 (also Appendix); Note on by Dr. Carpenter, 82 ; Thickened Walls of, 66; Preservation of, 100 ; Pores filled with Calcite, 97, 109; with Pyroxene, 108; with Serpentine, 101 ; with Dolomite, 109 ; in Limestone, 110; Defective Specimens of, 113 ; how Mineralized, 102, 116 ; its Contemporaries, 127 ; Acervuline Variety of, 135 ; Variety *Minor* of, 135 ; Acadianum, 140 ; Bavaricum, 148 ; Localities of, 166 ; Harmony of with other Fossils, 171 ; Summary vidence relating to, 176.

Faulted Eozoon, 182.
Foraminifera, Notice of, 61.

INDEX.

Fossils, how Mineralized, 93.
Fusulina, 74.

Glauconite, 100, 125, 220.
Graphite of Laurentian, 18, 27.
Greensand, 99.
Grenville, Eozoon of, 38.
Gümbel on Laurentian Fossils, 124; on Eozoon Bavaricum, 141.

Hastings, Rocks of, 57.
History of Discovery of Eozoon, 35.
Honeyman, Dr., referred to, 140.
Hunt, Dr. Sterry, referred to, 35; on Mineralization of Eozoon, 115; on Silurian Fossils infiltrated with Silicates, 121; on Minerals of the Laurentian, 123; on Laurentian Life, 27; his Reply to Objections, 199.
Huronian Rocks, 9.

Intermediate Skeleton, 64.
Iron Ores of Laurentian, 19.

Jones, Prof. T. Rupert, on Eozoon, 42.

King, Prof., his Objections, 184.

Labrador Felspar, 13.
Laurentian Rocks, 7; Fossils of, 130; Graphite of, 18, 27; Iron Ores of, 19; Limestones of, 17.
Limestones, Laurentian, 17; Silurian, 98.
Localities of Eozoon, 166.
Loftusia, 164.
Logan, Sir Wm., referred to, 36; on Laurentian, 24; on Nature of Eozoon, 57; Geological Relations of Eozoon, 48; on Additional Specimens of Eozoon, 52.
Loganite in Eozoon, 36, 102.
Lowe, Mr., referred to, 38.
Long Lake, Specimens from, 91.
Lyell, Sir C., on Eozoon, 234.

Madoc, Specimens from, 132.
Maps of Laurentian, 7, 16.
MacMullen, Mr., referred to, 37.
Metamorphism of Rocks, 13, 34.
Mineralization of Eozoon, 101; of Fossils, 93; Hunt on, 115.

Nicholson on Stromatopora, 165.
Nummulites, 73.
Nummuline Wall, 43, 65, 106, 176, 181.

Objections answered, 169, 188.

Parkeria, 164.
Petite Nation, 20, 43.
Pole Hill, Specimens from, 121.
Proper Wall, 43, 65, 106, 176, 181.
Preservation of Eozoon, 93.
Protozoa, their Nature, 59, 207.
Pseudomorphism, 200.
Pyroxene filling Eozoon, 108.

Red Clay of Pacific, 222.
Red Chalk, 222.
Reply to Objections, 167, 188.
Receptaculites, 162.
Robb, Mr., referred to, 120.
Rowney, Prof., Objections of, 184.

Serpentine mineralizing Eozoon, 102.

Silicates mineralizing Fossils, 100, 103, 121, 220.
Silurian Fossils infiltrated with Silicates, 121.
Steinhag, Eozoon of, 146.
Stromatopora, 37, 156.
Stromatoporidæ, 165.
Supplemental Skeleton, 64.

Table of Formations, 6.

Trinity Cape, 10.
Tubuli Explained, 66, 106.
Varieties of Eozoon, 135, 236.
Vennor, Mr., referred to, 46, 57.
Wentworth Specimens, 91.
Weston, Mr., referred to, 20, 40, 162.
Wilson, Dr., referred to, 36.
Worm-burrows in the Laurentian, 133, 139.

www.ingramcontent.com/pod-product-compliance
Lightning Source LLC
Chambersburg PA
CBHW032133230426
43672CB00011B/2326